PONY THE ANNUAL 2018

INSIDE YOUR ANNUAL...

Published by DJ Murphy (Publishers) Ltd, Marlborough House, Headley Road, Grayshott, Surrey GU26 6LG

Who did what in PONY – The Annual
Contributors Tilly Berendt, Emma Duncan, Rachel Dyke, Georgia Guerin, Jessica Lewis, Victoria Rea, Lucy Turner
Design Adam Witt

PONY magazine is published every four weeks. To find out more about PONY magazine, visit ponymag.com

Printed by Graphicom via dell'Industria – 36100 Vicenza, Italy

ISBN 978-0-9928279-4-6

8
20
50
58
72
16
Make
Look out for the pages with this star and try our fab makes

Eventing LEGENDS

Eventing is the ultimate horsey challenge, with riders taking part in dressage, showjumping and cross-country. Find out about the legends of this dare-devil sport

ANDREW NICHOLSON

Andrew's a Kiwi eventer who's ridden in six Olympic Games, winning three medals. He's won Burghley five times, Badminton once and holds the record for the highest number of Badminton completions – a whopping 37!

Most famous horse: Avebury

Andrew and Avebury are the only combination to have won Burghley Horse Trials three years in a row.

LUCINDA GREEN

Lucinda Green started riding when she was four years old, but didn't get her own horse until she was given Be Fair for her 15th birthday. The pair went on to win Badminton together and competed at the 1976 Olympics.

Most famous achievement...

She won Badminton Horse Trials six times on six different horses – which has never been done since!

MICHAEL JUNG

German eventer Michael Jung has won almost everything there is to win. He's the reigning Olympic, World and European Champion, and was the second rider to win the Rolex Grand Slam of Eventing.

Most famous horse:
La Biosthetique-Sam FBW
Sam's won two Olympic gold medals and is the only horse to have been placed in the top five an impressive 10 times at four-star level – that's the toughest level in the world!

WILLIAM FOX-PITT

William's been on the British team for more than 20 years. He's won Burghley a record six times and Badminton twice. He's won at the highest four-star level 14 times – something no one else has done!

Most famous horse: Tamarillo
Tamarillo won both Badminton and Burghley during his career, as well as a silver Olympic medal. A clone of Tamarillo was born in 2013.

MARK TODD

New Zealander Mark Todd needs no introduction, having been at the top of the sport for more than 40 years! He's won Badminton four times and Burghley five times, competed in seven Olympic Games and holds five Olympic medals!

Most famous achievement...
He won Badminton Horse Trials on his first attempt in 1980 and most recently won in 2011 aged 55 – the longest spread of wins in Badminton history!

PIPPA FUNNELL

Pippa Funnell is a super-successful British eventer, winning Badminton three times, Burghley once and holding five European gold medals. She's also a three-time Olympic medallist!

Most famous achievement...
In 2003 she became the first to win the Rolex Grand Slam of Eventing – winning at Badminton, Burghley and Kentucky consecutively.

MARY KING

Mary King is a horsey household name. Having learnt to ride on a vicar's pony, she proved her talent to work her way up through the levels.

Most famous achievement...
She holds three Olympic, three World Championship and five European Championship medals – that's a lot of medals!

ACE CROSS-COUNTRY!

Whether you're trying your hand at eventing or want to give hunter trials a go, read our winner's guide to getting a clear round!

Cross-country is all about confidence. To win, you need to be able to jump different kinds of solid objects, have an adjustable canter and be aware of your speed. There are loads of things you can practise while out hacking and cross-country schooling to put you on a winning streak before you get to a competition, as well as things to remember on the big day!

Fit for purpose

Before you think about going to a competition, your pony needs to be fit. Hacking is a great way to improve fitness without getting bored in the school. Build up your hacks gradually to include longer periods of trot and canter work. Walking and trotting up hills is also a great way to build fitness, as it encourages your pony to work properly and push from his hindquarters.

TOP TIP

Think about the ground you're riding on. Cantering on hard, rutted ground can damage your pony's legs and make him sore.

STRETCH IT OUT

It's a useful skill to be able to lengthen and shorten your pony's canter stride when you're going XC so you can make sure he's balanced and prepared to jump, as well being easily able to gallop on between fences.

To **shorten** his stride...

- half-halt to keep him focused and prepare him for the transition
- wrap your legs around his sides to keep him moving forwards
- sit up tall, bring your shoulders back and close your hands around the reins to control his energy

To **lengthen** his stride...

- soften your contact and allow your hands to move forwards slightly
- squeeze him forward with your legs into your hands

Shorten and lengthen your canter stride

TOP TIP

You can practise this on a hack, XC schooling, or even in the arena – try lengthening your pony's stride down the long sides and shortening it on the short sides. Remember to ride the exercise on both reins!

Turn over for top tips on tackling steps!

PRACTICE MAKES PERFECT

Going XC schooling with your instructor is the best way to get ready for a competition. It'll give you the opportunity to ride different types of fences, so you know what to expect on a course. As well as jumping simple logs, tiger traps and pheasant feeders, you're likely to come across other types of fences, including...

Water – at lower levels you'll just be expected to splash in and out, but in more difficult courses you may need to drop in or jump out. If your pony's not used to riding through water, ride it in walk first, then trot.

Ditches – approach ditches slowly to give your pony a chance to understand the question. Keep your eyes up, looking to the other side of the ditch, and encourage him over with your legs. Some ponies jump extra-big over ditches, so be ready to go with him!

Steps – you might be asked to ride these up or down. When you're jumping down steps, push your shoulders back and look up and ahead. Make sure to soften your hands to let the reins slide through your fingers slightly as your pony drops down. When you're jumping up steps, think of them as a normal fence, but remember to stay straight over all of them!

TOP TIP

Landings and getaways from fences are an easy place to make up your time. Push your pony on as you're landing from each fence before praising him. If you pat him before pushing him on, you'll lose valuable seconds.

Competition time!

It's super-exciting to go competing, but make sure you stay focused and remember everything you've practised in your schooling sessions – as well as the rules!

In most XC competitions, each refusal is worth 20 penalties, with the fourth refusal on course resulting in elimination. Three refusals at the same fence also causes elimination. A rider fall is 65 penalties, and a second fall is elimination.

Every second counts

XC competitions are timed, but it's not the fastest pony and rider who wins! Some courses will be timed throughout, while others have a timed section over a few fences. The clear round closest to the optimum time wins.

One day events often tell you the optimum completion time, but hunter trials might have a bogey time, where you won't know the specific time. A forward-going, steady canter is generally best, but the main thing is to jump round safely – even if this means going slightly slower.

First things first

A good warm-up is key to a good XC round. Make sure your pony's muscles have loosened up with a walk and trot on both reins, letting him stretch through his neck. You can practise lengthening and shortening his canter stride, as well as doing plenty of transitions, to keep him focused.

Start over a small, inviting fence to warm-up, before moving onto a bigger one. If you're eventing, keep your warm-up relatively short, as your pony will have already competed in dressage and showjumping.

Get into position

Your position around a cross-country course should be slightly different to your normal showjumping one. You're travelling faster and over longer distances, so it's easier for you and your pony if you're out of the saddle. Push your weight down into your heels and lift your body slightly up and forwards. Roll your shoulders up and back, keep a steady contact and look ahead to your fence. As well as putting you in a secure position, you'll find your pony naturally opens up his canter, too.

Enjoy yourself!

You've put in the hard work and practice, so the main thing to remember when you're out on course is to enjoy yourself! Keep smiling and jumping confidently. You'll have a red rosette in no time at all!

WHY DOES HE DO THAT?

It can sometimes feel like your pony has a few naughty or annoying habits, but there's a reason behind everything

It can be a bit difficult to understand exactly why your pony behaves the way he does. But it's important to think about why he's behaving like that because there's a reason behind every move he makes. Read on to find solutions to some common behaviour problems.

EXCITING TIMES

● **What he does...** You're trying to put travel boots on to get ready for a show and your pony just won't stand still.

● **Why he does it...** Ponies love routine! They know everything from when to expect their dinner to when it's time to come in from the field. So if something happens to disrupt their routine, such as preparing for a show, they can to become excited, stressed and trickier to manage.

● **What you can do...** Try to stay as calm and relaxed as possible, and allow yourself plenty of time to get your pony ready.

You can practise getting ready to travel, without actually taking him out. This can help him feel that it's something normal and not a sign that something super-exciting is about to happen.

FRIENDS FIRST

● **What he does...** He refuses to leave the yard on his own or tries to follow other ponies you meet while out hacking, which is known as napping.

● **Why he does it...** Ponies are herd animals, so are really social and find safety in numbers. Your pony will feel happiest when he has a friend with him to keep him company, which means that if you're leaving the yard on your own or going a different way to his friends on a hack, he might not been too keen.

● **What you can do...** It's important not to get too cross with him, as this is a natural response. Napping isn't something that can be stopped quickly and it'll take time to build his confidence. Reassure him, look up, ride positively, keep your leg firmly on and reward him when he does as you've asked.

FEELING SPOOKY

● **What he does...** He suddenly spooks or backs away snorting at something hidden in the hedge.

● **Why he does it...** Although the plastic bag may seem perfectly harmless to you, your pony sees it as a potential danger. Ponies don't think in the same way people do – we think before we react, whereas ponies react first and think after because they're flight animals, which means they run away from danger rather than turn and face it. You might find that once your pony has spooked or backed away, he'll have another look.

● **What you can do...** It's important not to tell your pony off, but reassure him everything's okay. Remember, ponies have better senses than we do, so he might be picking up on something you can't see or hear. Give him time, reassure him and, when he's feeling more relaxed, ask him to move forwards.

WHAT A BLOW OUT

● **What he does...** Your pony puffs himself out to make his barrel as big as possible while you're trying to do up his girth!

● **Why he does it...** Having something pulled tight around his belly can be uncomfortable, especially if you attempt to do your girth up as tightly as possible straightaway.

● **What you can do...** Use the first holes on each side and then gradually tighten the girth one hole at a time. This should make it more comfortable for your pony and he'll feel happier about having his girth done up.

DITCH THE ITCH

● **What he does...** After a sweaty workout your pony might try to rub his head on you.

● **Why he does it...** If you've ever had an itch you can't scratch then you'll know how he feels! Sweat become really uncomfy when it dries, especially where tack sits. It's bad manners to rub his head on you, and while it may seem funny at first, after a while it can become a habit and he'll expect to be able to use you as a scratching post every time – not cool!

● **What you can do...** Make sure you groom your pony thoroughly where his tack sits before you ride, and then again afterwards. He'll appreciate the itch relief and won't feel the need to push you over while trying to scratch his itchy head.

FUN WITH FRIENDS

● **What he does...** He gets super-strong, forward and excitable when hacking with friends.

● **Why he does it...** If you know you're going to spend a day out with your friends, you're likely to get a bit excited. It's the same for your pony. Going for a hack with a few of his pals is super-fun, and often speedy. He might show his excitement in a few different ways, such as throwing in a couple of bucks or by getting a bit strong.

● **What you can do...** The more regularly your pony hacks out with his friends the better he'll behave each time. Begin by riding with just one other person on an experienced pony. You can start by riding in the school together and then go for a short hack. Doing this regularly will help to teach your pony that riding with friends isn't a reason to get silly because it happens all the time.

SNACK TIME

● **What he does...** Your pony is partial to a snack or two while out hacking. He takes any opportunity he can to snack on a small tree branch or dive for some of the long lush grass!

● **Why he does it...** Ponies are grazing animals, which means they've evolved to eat small amounts of food almost all the time (and they like it that way!). So, it's a natural response for him to see food and try to eat it.

● **What you can do...** Keep him moving and use half-halts and transitions to encourage him to focus on you. Remember, hacks can be used to school your pony as well as having fun. Plus, by keeping him listening to what you're asking him to do, he's much less likely to be thinking about his stomach!

Make

ORIGAMI PONY BOOKMARKS!

Never lose your page with these super-cute pony bookmarks! Why not make a whole herd?

You'll need...

- ✔ origami paper
- ✔ pencil
- ✔ scissors
- ✔ glue
- ✔ googly eyes (optional)

TOP TIP Use whatever colour paper you'd like. Choose a fun pattern like ours, or why not match the colour to your fave pony? You can cut out markings such as a blaze or star and stick them on.

HOW TO DO IT

1. Fold the sheet of paper in half diagonally from corner to corner, to make a triangle. Keep the pattern on the outside.

2. Fold the bottom two points up to the top corner of the triangle, creating a diamond shape.

TOP TIP If you don't have any origami paper, cut normal A4 paper into a square.

3. Re-open the paper into a triangle, and fold the near side of the top point down to the bottom.

4. With the paper back in its diamond shape, fold down the tips on each side – these will be the ears.

5. Fold the tips backwards, tucking them inside the folded paper so the ears are showing.

6. Take another sheet of paper and draw on a forelock shape, triangles for the inner ears and circles for the nostrils.

7. Cut them out and stick them on your bookmark with some googly eyes. There you have it – a super-cute pony!

8. Tuck your origami pony onto the corner of your book to save your page for next time.

TOP TIP If you don't have googly eyes, you can use white and black paper or a pen to make your own.

BEST OF BRITISH BREEDS

NEW FOREST

We venture south to meet the talented New Forest pony

FAST FACTS

Height: 12–14.2hh
Colour: Usually bay, chestnut or grey. Piebald, skewbald and cremello colourings aren't permitted
Place of origin: Hampshire
The pony for you if... you daydream about scooping the red rosettes at Pony Club camp

New Forest ponies are one of the most popular native breeds, as they can turn a hoof to any task and come in a size to suit almost every rider.

Picture perfect

The ideal New Forest pony is considered a working type, meaning that his conformation should help him to carry a heavy weight, jump and tackle tricky terrain. They have sloping shoulders and strong, well-built quarters. They have a good depth of girth and aren't mega wide, which means they can take an adult rider's longer legs without being too wide for a smaller child. Their movement is active, but it's not as flashy as some breeds, such as the Dales pony. Smaller ponies (138cm and below) are shown as type A, and larger ponies (over 138cm) are shown as type B.

DID YOU KNOW?

The New Forest is kept under control by the feral ponies living there – they graze on the plants that would otherwise take over the forest.

In the history books

There have been wild ponies living in the New Forest since the end of the last Ice Age – that's more than 11,000 years! In fact, scientists have found fossils that indicate ponies might have been living in the area since 50,000 BC – pretty impressive stuff!

In 1066, William the Conqueror began the tradition of opening up the land for common use. For several centuries afterwards, New Forest ponies were used as pack ponies (to carry things) and even cavalry mounts in some European battles. In the 19th Century, Arab and Thoroughbred blood was introduced to add speed and the ponies became a popular racing breed.

The New Forest pony comes from the New Forest in Hampshire, on the south coast of England.

DID YOU KNOW?

Feral ponies in the New Forest aren't actually wild – they're all owned by locals, known as Commoners, and looked after by people called Agisters, each responsible for a specific section of the Forest.

FUNKY FORESTERS

Pony round-ups, known as drifts, are held in late summer to give the Agisters, or caretakers, a chance to check the ponies' health. A special design is then cut into the pony's tail so everyone knows which Agister looks after him. Cool, huh?

Ace all-rounders

New Forest ponies are known for being great at a variety of disciplines, and they're a popular choice for Pony Club activities. They're handy jumpers, so they can make fab eventers as they're so bold and sure-footed. New Forests also have their own special competition – the ponies can take part in a special point-to-point race across the Forest, held each year on Boxing Day. Competitors are told the starting and finishing point of the race the day before but, unlike other races, there's no set track to get to the end! This means that riders who know the Forest well have an advantage, as they can choose a clever route and are able to rely on their tough ponies to make easy work of galloping and jumping through the varying terrain and treacherous bogs.

HORSE SPORTS

VAULTING

Are you a pony-mad dancing diva? Why not give equestrian vaulting a go!

VAULTING VOCAB

Kur – freestyle competition
Pas-de-deux – pairs competition
Vault on – mounting
Scissors – handstand
Swing off – dismount

First introduced in the USA, vaulting is a fun combination of horseback dance and gymnastics. Competitors perform a series of different routines while their horse is lunged on a 15m circle. The sequences are judged on a scale of one to 10, with extra marks awarded for the horse's movement and behaviour. Competitions often take place over a number of days, as riders can compete as individuals, pairs and teams.

DID YOU KNOW?

Vaulting can be traced back as far as the Greek and Roman times when soldiers practised vaulting exercises as part of their military training.

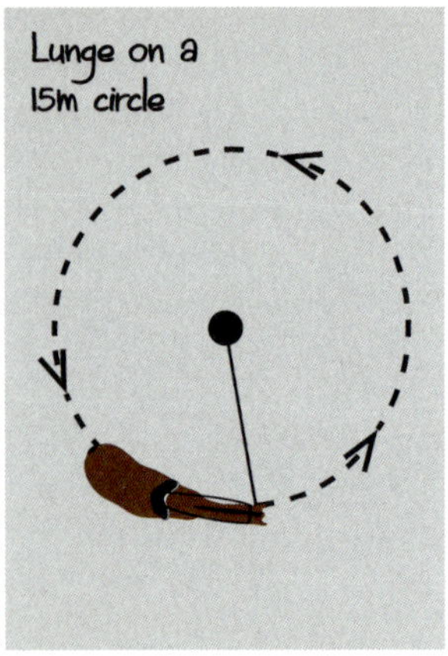

The low-down

Vaulting aims to test the rider's balance, co-ordination, strength and creativity, as well as their relationship with teammates and their horse. Vaulters have to complete a compulsory routine, riding in either walk, trot or canter. The difficulty and pace of this performance depend on the competition level. After completing the required sequence of exercises, riders showcase their freestyle routine, which gives them a chance to show off their creative side!

PONY magazine recommends you wear an up-to-standard riding hat at all times when mounted

DID YOU KNOW?

Vaulting routines are nearly always performed on the left rein but at home vaulters practise in both directions to stay even and balanced.

The gear

Unlike other equestrian events, vaulting horses don't wear a saddle. Instead, the riders perform using a thick back pad and surcingle, which has handles to help perform certain moves, as well as leather loops called cossack stirrups for extra stability. The horses also wear a regular bridle and side reins to help keep a consistent circle.

Dress code

Every few years the FEI releases new regulations for competition dress codes. Vaulters generally wear very tight-fitting uniforms so they don't get caught while they're performing. Most competitors wear super-snazzy, brightly coloured unitards!

DID YOU KNOW?

Vaulting is the only horsey sport where men and women are separated in individual competitions.

Official Status

Vaulting is an official FEI discipline, and it featured in the 1924 Olympics. The main international vaulting competitions are the FEI World Equestrian Games, which are held every four years, and the annual FEI World Cup.

Get involved!

Vaulting is an increasingly popular equestrian sport, with more than 25 clubs around the UK. Lots of groups offer trial days, so why not find a nearby club and get involved?

QUIZ!

What's that?

Have you ever come across a weird item of tack and not known what it was? Now's the time to test your knowledge!

1. What's a Weymouth bit?

- A It's an old fashioned bit that's only used for driving
- B It's one of two bits used with a double bridle
- C It's a type of pelham only used for really strong ponies

2. What would you use a crupper for?

- A To stop a saddle moving forwards
- B It's a special kind whip used for hunting
- C It stops your pony eating while being ridden

3. What are roundings?

- A Leather straps that attach to pelham bits so you can ride with one set of reins
- B It's the name for the D-shaped bits of metal on your saddle
- C It's another name for a curb chain

4. Where would you fit a sausage boot and what's it used for?

- A It goes around the hock and it stops your pony getting sores when he lies down
- B It's designed for riders to help support their ankles
- C It's fitted around your pony's pastern and stops him damaging his elbow when he's lying down

5. You've probably heard of a running and a standing martingale, but what's an Irish martingale?

- **A** It's what you call a running martingale that's attached to a breastplate
- **B** It attaches to the reins to stop them from going over your pony's head
- **C** It's a combination of a running and a standing martingale and is only used for showjumping

6. What's the bit in the picture below called?

- **A** Cheltenham gag
- **B** Eggbutt snaffle with cheek pieces
- **C** French link snaffle

7. What's a lungeing cavesson, and what would you use it for?

- **A** It's used for lungeing and is the correct name for the long lunge whip
- **B** It's a type of noseband, used for dressage
- **C** It's a special headcollar with rings on the noseband to attach a lunge rein to

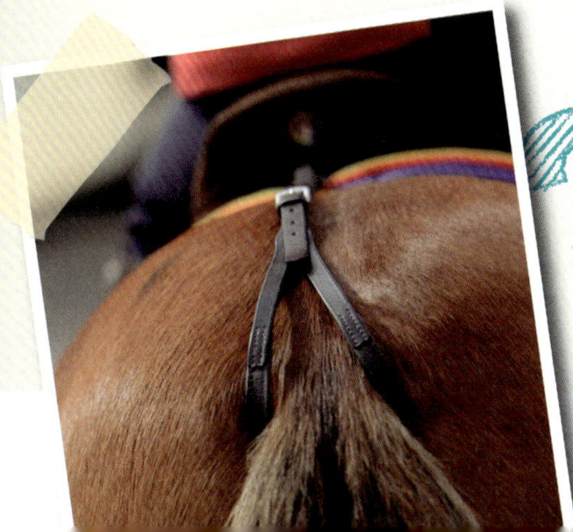

8. What's the difference between a breastplate and a breastgirth?

- **A** A breastplate is attached to the girth through the front legs and the Ds on the saddle. A breastgirth attaches to the sides of the girth and has leather straps that sit over the neck
- **B** A breastgirth is sometimes used in cross-country in case your girth gives way. Breastplates help stop your saddle sliding back
- **C** Breastgirths are only used for showjumping and breastplates are only allowed for eventing

9. What's a poll guard and when would you use it?

- **A** It's a special piece of soft material that covers heavy wooden poles to stop your pony injuring himself while jumping
- **B** It's a kind of hat that protects your pony's head while he's travelling
- **C** It's a bit of material that can be fixed to the frame of your pony's stable door in case he hits his head

10. What is a bradoon?

- **A** It's nothing to do with ponies and is an old type of money
- **B** It's an old-fashioned term for a bridle used in the army
- **C** It's one of the bits used when riding in a double bridle

Turn to page 100 to find out how you got on!

A NIGHT IN THE WILD

Eric lives with his owner, Laura, in the New Forest but he knows he's different to his friends. Will meeting his extended family in Exmoor make him happy?

Eric loved it when Laura took him for a hack in the New Forest. He'd lived on a yard there since he was born and he especially liked being out in the open. All his pals at the yard were New Forest ponies and a lot of them were family – brothers and sisters, even. They did everything – dressage, showjumping, showing – and were all pretty cool. But Eric wasn't like them. He was different. The New Forests never mentioned it, but he knew. He was much shorter and rounder, although pretty speedy when he wanted to be. Every night when Laura put Eric in his stable, he dreamed of living on Exmoor, playing with other Exmoor ponies who were just like him. Apart from that, Eric didn't want for anything. He loved Laura and she adored him, tending to his every need. But there were still times when Eric felt different and missed Exmoor, or at least the idea of it, because he'd never actually been there.

Eric had thought about leaving his home in the New Forest a couple of times, but he knew the journey to Exmoor was really long and, although he felt like he'd be able to walk for days and days if it meant seeing his family, he definitely didn't know the way. Plus, Laura's yard owner had escape-proofed the whole place after Cherry, a pony in his field, had been getting in some extra showjumping practice at night. So, if he was going to try, he needed to come up with a clever plan.

Eric and Laura

Plan in action

One sunny summer's day, Laura walked around the corner with his tack and called to her friends, "I'm just taking Eric for a hack, see you later!". This was it. Eric's chance had arrived. He stood quietly while Laura plaited his mane and tacked him up, calming his nerves. His mind started wandering and he thought about how much he'd miss Laura, but he came back to his senses just in time. As she put his saddle on, he puffed himself right out – this plan was only going to work if his girth was a little loose. "Blimey Eric, what have you been eating?" Laura asked as she tried to do his girth up.

They left the yard and went out onto the forest towards Laura's favourite track. After about 10 minutes she asked him to canter. It was now or never – Eric waited until he got to a bit of soft ground, dropped his shoulder and swerved to the left. He didn't want to hurt Laura, but he needed to be sure she'd come off. Luckily, because he was never normally naughty, so Laura was taken by surprise and slipped straight out of the saddle. Eric looked back to check she was okay and, when he saw she was already on her feet, he cantered off, accidentally splattering her with mud. He headed towards a wooded area to give himself a chance to gather his racing thoughts, ready to start his journey to Exmoor.

In disguise

Eric wandered across the forest for an hour or so and soon realised he had no idea which way to go. He'd passed a few groups of wild New Forest ponies and, although he'd never spoken to any before, he decided to approach the next herd he came across, hoping they'd be able to give him a good start.

He had heard that the ponies who lived on the forest lived a fairly wild life, and weren't very welcoming to human-kept ponies, but this is where Eric's plan really came into play. Because his saddle was a little loose, he was able to reach around, tuck his nose under the saddle flap, tug up the girth straps and undo them. "Genius!" he thought to himself. He used a tree to pull off his bridle, ruffled up his plaits on the bark, and had a good roll in the stinkiest bog he could find. His disguise was complete, Eric the newly rustic-looking Exmoor was ready.

The encounter

It wasn't long before he came across a group of wild New Forest ponies. They were bigger and rougher-looking than he'd realised (Laura had never let him get this close), but Eric crept up to them anyway. "You can do it," he told himself, "if you want to get back to your family, you need to be brave".

"Errm, excuse me... hello? I'm Eric and I'm on my way to, er, Exmoor. I was just wondering whether you knew which way to go?" Eric said in his best fake confident voice. The ponies looked up and turned to face him. "Eric?! What kind of a name is that? Oi, Bracken, have you seen this?"

"Yeah, mate. He's not fooling me with a plaited mane and shiny shoes, no matter how much mud he's rolled in. I don't know what he thinks he's doing out here, talking to us?! And Exmoor? That's miles away!" This wasn't what Eric had expected. He'd heard the wild ponies didn't have any manners, but he'd hoped it was a myth and they'd really be more like the human-kept ponies at home.

"So... do you know the way?" Eric asked again, "Or can I stay with you until I find someone who does?" It was getting dark and Eric had never spent a day on his own, let alone a night, and he didn't like the idea of this much even if it meant staying with Bracken.

"We know you're not from round here, you're way too posh to fool us. You can't stay here, and you'll never make it to Exmoor on those little legs," Bracken retorted. Eric was hurt. His differences hadn't mattered to anyone at the yard, and he'd never been left out or excluded. He turned around with a tear in his eye and his head low, and walked away.

> "Eric had a good roll in the stinkiest bog he could find. His disguise was complete"

Going solo

Eric walked for what felt like hours. It must have been a long time because it was now completely dark. He still didn't know where he was going, and he didn't recognise where he was anymore, either, because he'd never been out on the forest at night. Then, as if things couldn't get any worse, it began to rain. There wasn't much in the way of shelter nearby, so Eric lay down and huddled under a spiky gorse bush. "This isn't a patch on my stable," he thought. He was all alone, lost and had nowhere to go. He thought about Laura. She would've made it home ages ago and was probably going out of her mind with worry. "What have I done?" he thought. He had been selfish to think that going to Exmoor would make everything better, and he'd never been as unhappy as he was now. He realised that his friends treated him like family even though they weren't and, as well as Laura, that was all he could ever need. It didn't take him long to decide what to do next. "I'm going home!" he declared to himself.

Heading home

Eric couldn't wait for the sun to come up. As soon as there was the tiniest amount of light, he was up on his feet and looking around for a clue as to where he was. When he worked it out, he couldn't believe it. He was at the end of the disused runway, not that far away from home at all! He must have gone in a complete circle! Eric set off down the runway at top speed, just like he did when he was racing his friends on a hack. He cantered all the way home – he'd never gone so far at such speed – Laura would be impressed if she knew. Thinking of Laura, he crossed his hooves that she wouldn't be too cross with him for running off.

He rounded the final corner a little too fast, skidding into the yard just as the other ponies were getting their breakfast. "Eric! You're back! Laura's going to be so relieved to see you!" Cherry called over the cheering and stamping made by the other ponies. Eric's stable door was open, so he trotted in and waited as if everything was normal. Laura must have heard the commotion because she came running round the corner. She stopped for a moment when she saw Eric, then sprinted into his stable, flung her arms around his neck and started to sob with relief and happiness. "I can't believe it, I thought you were never coming home, I've been worrying all night." Eric wanted to tell her he was sorry, so curled his neck around her to give her his best hug. "Never leave me again," pleaded Laura.

"Don't you worry about that," Eric thought, "I'm going nowhere. This is the best home ever."

IN IT TO *win it*

Phoebe can't wait to do her first hunter trial with her sister. But it seems their ponies are even more competitive than the girls are!

Ruby and Gem
as **Phoebe and Lulu**

Bea and Lily
as **Hannah and Poppy**

Charlie
as **Prince**

Look at me go!
I'm getting the hang of this now.
Right, let's go and have a steady warm up.
Wow, Lulu feels great!
Poppy's super-keen, too!
Keep Lulu steady so you get a good approach, Phoebe!
You're the best pony ever, Lulu!

You're both ready for tomorrow. Good luck!
Thanks, Prince!
THE NEXT DAY...
I hope you've both had your beauty sleep!
We're going to have so much fun.
Remember, today's just about having fun.
Thanks, Hannah. I'm super-excited!
Just fun? Yeah, right!
We're in it to win it!
This is so much fun!
We've gone clear!
YAY!
WE'RE THE WINNERS!
Looks like all our practice paid off!
The end

HORSE SPORTS

POLOCROSSE

Do you have the guts to gallop down the pitch fighting off the opposition? Polocrosse could be for you!

Polocrosse is a fun, fast horse sport that's a mix of polo and lacrosse. Each rider carries a stick with a net on the end that's used to catch and carry the ball. It's a team game so the players pass to other members of their team to try to score goals.

DID YOU KNOW?

Polocrosse was first developed in Australia, but is now played all over the world.

Team tactics

Each team has six players, but only three are on the pitch at a time. Like polo, matches are broken up into six to eight minute chukkas, and there can be four, six or eight chukkas in a match. Three players in the team play one chukka while the other three wait on the sidelines, then they swap for the next chukka. Unlike polo, each player is only allowed to compete on one horse throughout the match.

YOU WILL NEED...

- ✓ riding helmet (that meets all current safety standards)
- ✓ sturdy riding boots
- ✓ coloured team tops
- ✓ polocrosse stick
- ✓ sponge rubber ball
- ✓ pony bandages
- ✓ overreach boots

Quick off the mark

The game begins in the centre of the field, with each team lining up behind their number one player – this is called the line out. The ball is then thrown onto the pitch and everyone races to get to it first. Once the ball's caught or scooped into a net, it's all about speed!

Remember this is a team game, so you'll need help from other players when racing for the goal. Throughout the game, it's also key to have control of both your pony and stick, as this will make turning, passing and scoring a lot easier.

Can I play on my pony?

Of course! Any pony can play polocrosse, although ponies who are fast, agile and responsive tend to make the best mounts. If your pony has these qualities you should definitely give polocrosse a try.

DID YOU KNOW?

Polocrosse was originally played indoors and riders could use the walls to bounce the ball back into play.

DID YOU KNOW?

Like netball, the three team members each have a section of the pitch that they play in. However, all competitors are allowed to ride in the centre of the field too.

Lets get started!

Although polocrosse has been an official Pony Club discipline since 2011, it's become more and more popular in the last couple of years. If your branch or centre doesn't have a team yet, why not speak to your instructor and set one up with a group of friends?

Badges on offer

There are two Pony Club competition badges to get your hands on! The Intro to Polocrosse badge is for less experienced members who have just started playing. But, once you understand the rules and are out competing, there's an advanced one, too.

The perfect SHOW DAY DIARY

Want to know the winning formula for a good day at a show? Megan and her pony, Izzy, reveal all

The day before...

Today is prep day! It's a chance to get everything sorted so that me and Izzy are all set for tomorrow morning – that way I can savour every last minute in bed because it will deffo be an early start!

3pm
I give Izzy a good groom, then bath her and wash her mane and tail. Detangling sprays are soooo handy!

4pm
I make sure I've got all my show kit ready – I always make a list so I don't forget anything.

5pm
Finally, I clean my boots and tack so they sparkle! Hopefully we'll catch the judge's eye.

The morning of...

Today's the day! This morning it's all about the final touches before it's time to leave.

6.30am
I check that Izzy's kept herself clean overnight. Then I give her another groom and spot-clean any stains she's managed to pick up.

7am
I always put Izzy in her best gear for a show (headcollar, rug, boots, everything!) because she needs to feel the part – even better if it matches!

7.30am
When I've packed my lorry with everything I need (note to self: Don't forget water, haynet, tack, grooming kit and my show gear), all I need to do is load Izzy and we're ready to go!

At the show...

We've made it! We're super-prepared and ready for action so now it's time to focus on my riding and enjoy myself!

8.30am
I arrive in plenty of time to tack up and do a final dirt check. Whatever Izzy thinks, I know it makes all the difference.

8.45am
I have a good warm-up. I like to make sure Izzy's relaxed and listening to me because there's such a different atmosphere at a show.

When we're in the class, it's time to pull out all our best moves that we've worked so hard on. But I don't worry if it's not perfect – it's mainly about having a good time with Izzy. Luckily today felt amazing!

My fave part of the day... snack time!

11:00
I make sure Izzy knows she's done well and I get my mum to take loads of pics – so important! Then, before we leave, I sponge Izzy off and put all her travel gear back on.

Make sure you get my best side, please!

9.25am
I always loosen Izzy's girth and make time to relax with her between classes or while we're waiting for results so she remembers it as a fun day out.

10.40am
The results are in and it's time to shine – the lap of honour is my fave!

Can we race?

Back at the yard...

Totally exhausted, I put everything away so everyone (especially Izzy) can have a well-earned rest.

I turn Izzy out for a good roll – she'll really appreciate it after her big day! Then all I have to do is unload and clear out the lorry, and I can go home and hang up my rosettes and wait for the photographer's photos to appear online.

Wahooo! Ohhhh yeah!

HAPPY AND ALERT

You'll recognise this expression if your pony's ears are pricked, his mouth and nostrils are relaxed, and his eyes are soft. This usually means he's relaxed, happy and aware of what's going on around him.

He might do this if he's watching the action on the yard or in the field, or maybe he's after the tasty treat he knows is in your pocket!

FACE TIME

Ever wondered what your fave pony's thinking? Become a pony whisperer and check out our guide to reading his facial expressions

Ponies have a total of 17 different facial expressions – that's more than dogs or chimpanzees! They create these expressions using the muscles around their mouth, nostrils, eyes and ears. Lots of these are very similar to human expressions, and you can tell a lot from them about what your fave pony's thinking.

ANGRY

It's best to avoid a pony who's looking like this! His ears will be pinned back against his head, with his nostrils and mouth tense and wrinkled. He might show the whites of his eyes, too.

Your pony might show this expression if he's arguing with his fieldmates or unhappy about something – for example, you've tightened his girth too sharply. It's often a warning to stay away, so make sure you don't enter his biting or kicking range.

SCARED OR NERVOUS

When your fave pony has this expression, his ears are pricked with his eyes wide and nostrils flared. This is how he looks if he's nervous – maybe he's seen or heard something he's not sure about in the distance.

Don't get cross with your pony if he looks like this – ponies can see and hear much better than you can, so you might not be able to work out what's upsetting him.

RELAXED

If your pony's relaxed, he'll lower his head, droop his ears slightly backwards or to the side, and his eyes might half-close. As his mouth relaxes, he might even have a droopy bottom lip!

Your pony will only relax if he's totally comfortable in his surroundings. He might do this if he's on the yard or in his stable after a ride or grooming session, or when he's turned out with his fieldmates who are on watch duty.

FLEHMEN RESPONSE

Despite what it looks like, your pony isn't laughing when he makes this face! It's called the Flehmen response, and he does it when he smells something unusual or interesting.

Ponies curl their upper lip and breathe in, which lets them detect the scent molecules in the air better. Your pony might do it if there's a new pony on the yard, or if he comes across an unknown smell or taste.

YAWNING

It's common for ponies to yawn, but it hasn't been proven just quite why they do it! Some people think it's a reaction to stress – for example, once they've worked out a threat isn't going to harm them, they yawn to release the tension. Others think ponies yawn in anticipation – such as when they're waiting for their dinner or before they're ridden.

It's also been noticed that ponies sometimes yawn when they're in pain – particularly abdominal pain. This is normally accompanied by other signs, such as colic symptoms.

Real life!

INTO THE UNKNOWN

When Beth took her pony, Bumble, exploring, they found themselves in a tricky situation. Would they make it home safe and sound?

I've always been into exploring and love to head out on Bumble for hours, just the two of us. Sometimes my friends come with us, but not often, as they get bored, tired and hungry, and want to head for home just as we get to an area I haven't been to before. But as much as they get bored of my epic rides, they always know who to ask for the best places to gallop!

The best bit about exploring with Bumble is he always knows the way home – if I lose my bearings, I just drop the reins and let him pick which way to go. To be honest, that part is just as much fun as finding new places to ride – having a bond with him where I trust him to get me home feels really special. We've had Bumble for years and Mum knows he'll look after me so she doesn't ever worry about us, plus she knows we're always home before dark. Until one day...

Adventure seeking

It was the summer holidays and the weather was awesome, so Bumble and I set out for an afternoon ride in the direction of the river, which has a shallow area that you can ride in and splash around. I hadn't explored very far on the other side, but it was the perfect day for it. Armed with a picnic and an apple for Bumble, we set off into the woods towards the long, sandy stretch that led to the river – Bumble's favourite place for a gallop.

With the sun beating down, we came to a stop at the water, puffing and swishing away the flies that had started to gather. Bumble didn't waste any time getting into the river for a drink and I let him have a paddle. Hot and sweaty, he began circling for a roll, so I laughed and called time on the fun – I wasn't up for getting soaked and Mum would have killed me if his saddle went in! I gave him a small nudge and he leapt up the bank onto the other side. It wasn't long before we were exploring new territory.

A magical surprise

It was a long walk down lots of narrow, almost invisible paths in the woods with nothing to see but hundreds of tall trees tightly packed together and I was beginning to think that this ride wasn't going to be very exciting. Just as I started to think about heading back, the woods opened out into the most incredible scenery. In front of us was an open corn field with a path running through it and to our right a huge hill that had little waterfalls running down it.

Excited at my find, I didn't know which way to go first, but after so much walking a good canter along the path through the crops was the most appealing option. Bumble must have thought the same, because he suddenly blasted off, me whooping and laughing as the corn that hung over the path whipped my face.

Once out of the field, a path appeared to the right that went in the direction of the hill – our next place to visit. It got really steep and rocky, but luckily the path zig-zagged across the hill so it was a bit easier for Bumble. I could hear splashing and gurgling, so I went in search of the little waterfalls I'd seen from the edge of the woods. Crashing against the rocks, they looked incredible with the sun glinting on the water droplets as they flew through the air. Other than a few small rabbits darting about, there was no one around and it felt like I'd found a magical wonderland.

Race against time

Thinking the girls at the yard wouldn't believe it and wondering whether I could talk them into coming here, my heart suddenly leapt into my mouth. I'd completely lost track of time and the sun was looking very low in the sky. I was miles away and there was no way I'd even be back to the river by dark, let alone home.

We needed to get back as quickly as possible. I could

have continued on down the hill to get back to the woods, which was the more direct route, but I didn't know whether the tracks would be passable or where we were going. If I turned around and went back the way we came, it would be longer, but at least Bumble and I knew where to go, so that's what we did.

Kicking on where I could to make up time, we were losing our race against the sunset and as we stepped into the woods we were plunged into darkness. I gave Bumble his head and let him choose where to go. I had no idea which path to take – they all looked the same. Walking on confidently, Bumble picked his way over the roots and fallen branches, only stumbling a couple of times, even though it was pitch black. It had felt like we'd been in the woods a long time earlier on, but this time it seemed never-ending.

I finally heard the gentle gurgling of the river, and threw my arms around Bumble's neck – this pony was incredible. Once we got across the river safely we'd be home and dry, as I knew the way back from there very well. All I had to get through after that was explaining myself to Mum.

> "Lying in the dark, I started to notice noises coming from deep in the woods"

No way out

As we got closer to the river and I could see it through the darkness, I realised it wasn't our shallow crossing. The bank was high and steep, and the water was moving quickly and looked deep. Bumble was hovering on the edge of the bank, unsure what to do and the ground started to crumble away under his feet. Even if we made it down the bank safely, there was no telling how deep the water was – getting into the river there wasn't an option.

I started to walk along the river to the left – we couldn't have been far from the crossing. But after what felt like a lot of walking, I still couldn't find a safe place to cross. Thinking it must have been the other way I walked back, but still nothing. The time had come when I'd have to ring Mum and confess that we were lost – she was going to go crazy.

Home for the night

I got my phone out but there was no signal and to my horror I only had 2% battery left. What now? I didn't dare to wander any further in the dark and get even more lost, so decided to set up camp and wait until it was light again. I found a thick bush to shelter against and snapped off several leafy branches to lie on.

Suddenly my tummy rumbled. Thankfully I still had my packed lunch to eat, so I tucked in. Poor Bumble only had an apple, although he found plenty to munch on at our camp site. I took off his saddle, but had to leave his bridle on in case I lost him, although I felt guilty because he'd been wearing it for so long. I took the reins over his head and clung onto them, lying on my hand for extra grip in case I nodded off.

I started to notice noises coming from deep in the woods. A twig snapped nearby. Was that Bumble or something else? Could it be something not very friendly? Who knows what could be living in there. My imagination began to run wild and I was seriously reconsidering camping out for the night.

A familiar sound

Lying in the woods, heart beating fast, I was keeping frozen still while listening out for any scary noises. Then Bumble's head suddenly shot up. What had he heard? Was something creeping up on us? Holding my breath while I listened hard, I couldn't hear anything. But Bumble was becoming more and more agitated.

Then I thought I heard a voice. I listened again. It was definitely a voice. Maybe even someone calling my name? I leapt up and put Bumble's saddle on, then climbed on board. Bumble insisted on marching off. Guessing he was heading for the voice, but at the same time scared of getting even more lost, I decided to give him his head and trust him.

The voice was getting louder and it sounded more and more like Mum. Then I saw what looked like torch lights moving on the other side of the river. Suddenly I recognised where I was. It was the crossing. I've never felt so relieved! Realising Mum was on the other side, along with my friends from the yard, Bumble and I trotted through the river and I leapt off into Mum's arms.

Safe at last

After a severe telling off from Mum for frightening her, next came all the questions about where I'd been and what had happened. Luckily for me, one of the other liveries at the yard had seen which direction I'd headed, so they knew roughly where to start looking for me when I didn't come home.

I'm not sure why Bumble didn't get me home – maybe he was tired after such a long ride or perhaps the dark threw him off. But one thing's for sure, in future I'll always let someone know where I'm going and I'll always have my phone fully charged, although I can safely say solo hacking won't be happening for a while!

You'll need...

- mixing bowl
- two greased and lined cake tins at least 23cm in diameter
- five eggs
- 365g butter
- 280g caster sugar
- 280g self-raising flour
- 170g icing sugar
- 1 tsp vanilla essence
- 1 tsp baking powder
- jam
- ready-to-use regal icing
- coloured regal icing
- black writing icing pen

Make A PONY CAKE!

Surprise your friends with a super-fun pony cake, great for birthday celebrations or just a treat

HOW TO DO IT

1. Beat 280g of butter and the caster sugar together until light and fluffy, then add the flour and mix well. Beat in the eggs, vanilla essence and baking powder. Once all the ingredients are thoroughly combined, tip the mixture into the tins. Bake in the oven at 180°C (gas mark 4) for about 30 minutes. They should be a light golden colour and springy to the touch.

TOP TIP You can use any flavour of sponge you'd like, such as chocolate, as the base of your pony cake.

TURN TO PAGE 101 FOR THE CAKE TEMPLATE

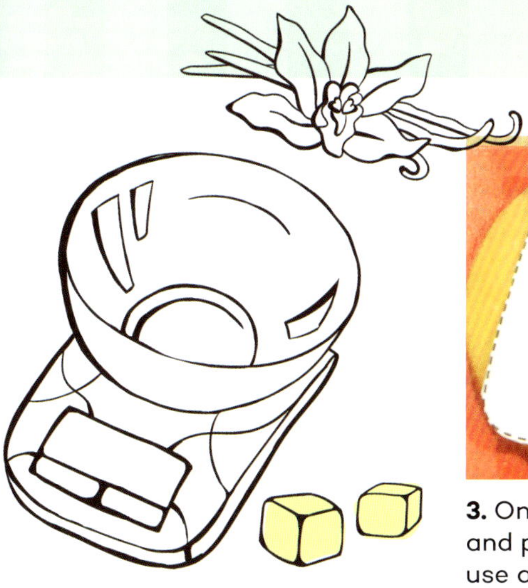

3. Once the cake is completely cool, take the pony head template and place it on top of one of the cakes. Ask an adult for help and use a knife to carefully cut around the template. Repeat for the second cake.

2. While the cake's cooling, make butter icing by combining 85g butter and 170g icing sugar. Add a few drops of vanilla essence for extra yumminess.

4. Carefully spread some jam on top of one of the cakes to glue the two sponges together. Place the second sponge on top, making sure the two cakes are perfectly lined up.

5. Once you're happy with the position of your sponges, spread the butter icing evenly over the top and sides of the cake. This will help the regal icing stick to the sponge.

6. Roll out the regal icing and drape it over the top. Gently push the icing onto the cake, making sure it's completely covered. You may need to cut a slit in the icing on the point of the ear and neck, so it can be folded over itself, leaving a neat line.

7. Cut away the extra icing and keep to one side, as you'll need this later!

TOP TIP Shaping the icing around the cakes can be fiddly, so ask an adult to help.

8. Take your coloured regal icing and roll out two pieces for the headcollar. Place the noseband on first, then the headpiece.

9. Once the headcollar is in place, use the writing icing pen to draw on a nostril and eye.

10. Finally, take the leftover regal icing and roll it into sausage shapes for the mane and forelock. Starting at the ears and moving down the neck, gently press the mane pieces into the cake. Finally, press the forelock pieces into place.

TOP TIP If the icing won't stick, use a drop of water to keep it in place.

BEST OF BRITISH BREEDS
DALES

Join PONY on a trip to the north of England as we meet the fab and flashy Dales pony!

FAST FACTS
Height: 14–14.2hh
Colour: Usually black, but can also be brown, bay, grey and, in rare cases, roan
Place of origin: Yorkshire
The pony for you if... you want a hardy all-rounder who can manage the most challenging of hacks

The largest of all the pony breeds native to the British Isles, the Dales pony is known for its distinctive black coat, abundant mane and tail, and flashy, high-stepping trot. Look familiar? That's because the Dales descended from the now-extinct Galloway pony – the same breed that the slightly smaller Fell pony came from. The Fell pony is the Queen's choice of mount – so if you ride a Dales, you'll practically be mounted on equine royalty!

DID YOU KNOW?
The Dales pony is officially considered endangered – it's believed that there are only around 1,500 of these fab ponies worldwide.

DID YOU KNOW?
There are still some Dales ponies roaming free in the eastern Pennines. On holiday in the Peak District? Keep your eyes peeled for ponies!

Purpose-built ponies

Nobody is quite sure when the Dales pony was first established as a breed, but as far back as Roman times there are references to hardy local ponies being used for the cavalry and in lead mines. The ponies were bred to be strong, hardy and intelligent, rather than to follow any breed standards. But, in the 18th and 19th centuries, the native ponies were bred with trotters to give the Dales its distinctive, expressive trot.

In the 20th Century, the Dales was called on for the Second World War effort because their incredible strength and bravery made them the perfect pack ponies, used to carry supplies and artillery on the battlefield. Unfortunately, their numbers dropped as a result, and fans of the beautiful breed had to work very hard to save it once the war ended.

Modern marvels

Nowadays, Dales ponies are still prized for their hardiness, but they tend to be put to different uses! Dales are popular all-rounders, and can be found dazzling the judges in the show ring. Because of their enviable strength, paired with a kind and brave nature, they're suitable for younger riders and adults. Their strong, sure-footed nature makes them fantastic for hacking, and they can easily cope with long distances and tricky terrain. They also easily take to pulling a trap, and are handy jumpers – talk about multi-talented!

The gold standard

The Dales pony is most commonly black, with a neat, pretty head and small ears. Their body is broad and muscular, and their legs are stocky with large hooves. Having short backs and sturdy bodies means they're extraordinarily strong for their size. They also have long, thick manes and tails and plenty of feathering on their legs – all this acts as a natural raincoat for the harsh Yorkshire winters!

Most Dales ponies don't have markings, but some may have a small star or snip, and a bit of white up to their fetlocks.

Fly THOSE FENCES

Follow our guide on how to jump different types of fences and you'll be flying around the course in no time!

One of the best things about showjumping is all the types of fences there are to jump. No one fence is the same and each will require a slightly different approach. Some need a forward canter while others require a steadier pace. Here are some of the main types of fences and how to tackle them...

Cross-poles

What is it? A cross-pole is made of two poles with opposite ends raised to form a cross shape. They're a great way to start warming up for jumping.

How to ride it... The centre where the two poles cross is the lowest point of the fence and where you should aim to jump. You can approach this fence in trot or canter in either direction.

Uprights

What is it? An upright is a single fence made of poles and sometimes a filler, too.
How to ride it... Although they're relatively easy to jump, it's important to ride uprights properly. You'll need a bouncy canter to help your pony jump well over the fence and clear it. Remember to look up and over the fence to your next one as you land.

Spreads

What is it? Also known as an oxer, a spread is made up of two uprights placed slightly apart to create one wider fence. Although they can look scary, spreads are actually easy for your pony to jump as they encourage him to round his back.
How to ride it... You'll need a confident, open canter to tackle this fence, so wrap your legs around your pony's sides to encourage him forward. Look up and ahead, and aim for the centre of the fence.

DID YOU KNOW?

Spreads can be parallel or ascending – the poles in a parallel are the same height, whereas on an ascending spread the back pole (on the landing side) is set slightly higher than the front one.

Combinations

What is it? A combination is two or more fences that are less than three strides apart from each other, such as a double. The fences will have the same number, but given an individual letter – for example, 4a and 4b.
How to ride it... Make sure you know how many strides your pony should take between each part of the combination, as this will help you prepare for jumping the next element. Ask for a forward, bouncy canter and approach the first element of the combination straight, aiming for the centre.

When you land, maintain a forward canter but don't rush, otherwise you'll have less time to prepare for the next fence. Make sure you keep the impulsion through the combination for a confident jump out because not having enough can result in a refusal or a run out.

TOP TIP

Remember, impulsion isn't the same as speed. Impulsion is the energy your pony needs to get himself over the jump.

> *"A combination is two or more fences that are less than three strides apart"*

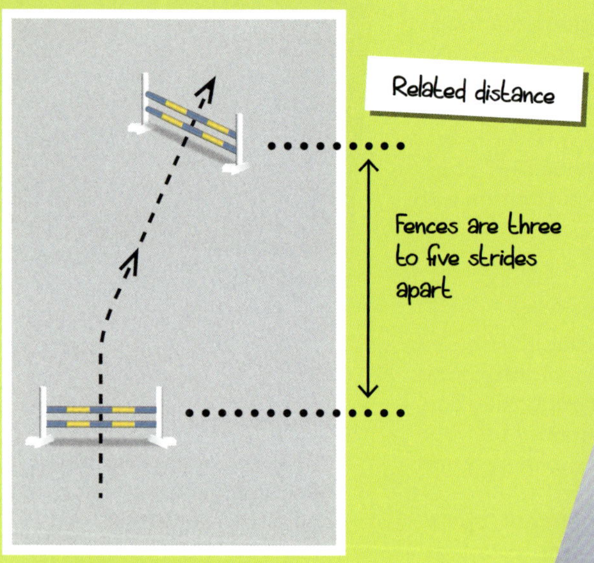

Related distances

What is it? A related distance is made up of a pair of differently numbered fences that are three to five strides apart. Related distances are similar to a combination and can be approached in the same way. However, the two fences might not be built in a straight line, but instead are on a slight bend known as a dog-leg.

How to ride it... It's important to walk the course and know what line you need to take to the second fence. Make sure that you have an even contact and stick to your planned route. As you're landing from the first fence, look over to the second to let your pony know where the next fence is.

Planks

What is it? This is just like an upright but made up of straight planks rather than rounded poles. Planks are sometimes supported by flat cups, which can make them easier to knock down.

How to ride it... As you approach, wrap your legs firmly round your pony's sides to keep straight and aim for the centre of the fence. Be careful not to approach too fast, as your pony needs enough time to get his hindquarters underneath him to make a good shape over the fence.

TOP TIP
If your pony isn't listening to you, come back to trot for a few strides before asking him to canter on again.

Fillers

What is it? Fillers are added underneath or to the sides of fences. Some ponies find them scary, as they can be colourful and designed in odd shapes or patterns.

How to ride it... Maintain a forward, bouncy canter and sit up tall. Wrap your legs tightly around his sides and ride positively. Fillers are designed to draw your eye and make you look down, so it's important to make sure that you're looking up and over the fence.

Skinnies

What is it? Skinnies are narrow fences. They look simple but can be tricky, as there's less of a jump to aim at.

How to ride it... A straight approach is vital to stop your pony being tempted to duck out the side. Make sure you've planned the line you're going to take before attempting to jump. Ask for a steady canter and maintain an even contact. Keep your legs pressed against his sides to help him stay straight and ride confidently.

Now you're ready to tackle any fence you meet, just remember to ride positively and have fun conquering those courses!

BARREL RACING

Speed-demons only! Barrel racing is a super-fast Western riding sport. Do you have what it takes?

DID YOU KNOW?

A good barrel horse has strength, agility and speed. Common barrel horse breeds include Thoroughbreds, Arabians and American Quarter Horses.

Originating in Texas, USA, barrel racing is a hugely popular sport across the whole of North America. Races are held at rodeo events and test the speed and skills of cowboys and girls. Rodeos often take place across several days, with hundreds of people competing – and plenty of prizes up for grabs!

Lucky clover

Barrel racing follows a clover leaf pattern around three barrels. Riders can decide whether to approach the left or right barrel first. They circle around it, then move on to the barrel on the other side and ride around it in the opposite direction. They finish off by riding around the top barrel, before galloping at full-speed through the finish!

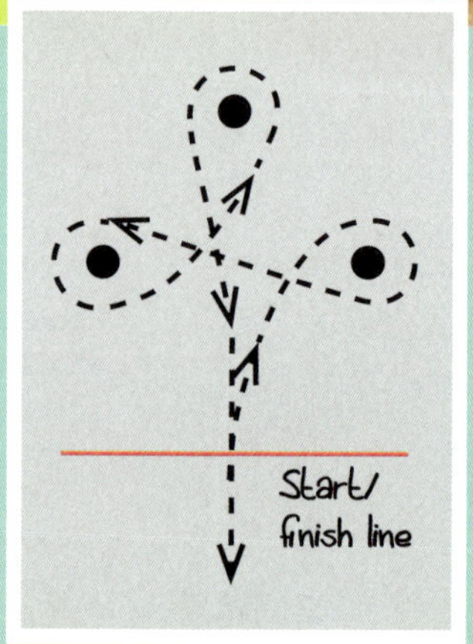

DID YOU KNOW?

Barrel racers enter the arena at a gallop, so they cross through the start and finish line at full speed.

DID YOU KNOW?

Barrel racing started out as a sport for women at male-dominated rodeo events in the early 1900s.

PONY magazine recommends you wear an up-to-standard riding hat when mounted at all times

Fast and furious

In barrel racing, speed is key, with the fastest time of the day taking home the trophy. If a rider or pony knocks over a barrel, a five-second time penalty is added, which usually pushes them down the rankings. Riders have a time limit of 60 seconds to complete the pattern – so you can't hang around. With winners decided by time differences of less than a second, it's nail-biting stuff!

Neck reining

Most Western-trained horses understand neck reining, which means that they're guided by the reins touching their neck, rather than direct contact through the bit.

Riders hold their reins in one hand and move the reins to the left of the horse's neck to turn left, and the opposite way to turn right. Riders hold the horn of the saddle with their other hand for stability as they turn around the barrels at speed.

Saddle up

Western tack is used for this sport, and many riders use special barrel racing saddles. These are lightweight, with a deep seat for added security. A breastplate is often used to help keep the saddle secure at high speeds. Tie-downs – similar to a standing martingale – are frequently used, too.

Dress to impress

Cowboy dress is a must at these events! Most riders wear jeans and a long-sleeved, western-style shirt, along with cowboy boots and a cowboy hat or helmet. Lots of riders wear bright colours, often matching their tack, to stand out from other competitors.

Showjumping LEGENDS

Showjumping requires speed and accuracy to win, and these legends have bucket loads of the skills needed to be champions

NICK SKELTON

Nick's first major win was the Junior European Championships in 1975 and 41 years later he took home the individual gold medal at the 2016 Olympic Games. He currently holds the British showjumping high jump record, which he set in 1978, clearing a whopping 2.32m!

Most famous horse: Big Star

Nick and Big Star stole the nation's hearts as they took home team gold in the 2012 Olympics and individual gold in the 2016 Olympics. Nick describes Big Star as the best horse he's ever ridden.

ELLEN WHITAKER

Ellen started competing when she was only five years old and first qualified for HOYS at the age of eight! With showjumping in her blood, she was a favourite sight at top showjumping competitions with her long, blonde ponytail and red show jacket!

Most famous horse: Ladina B

Ladina became famous for her talent in Puissance classes, winning at Olympia with Ellen in 2009. Ladina's excitable nature and huge jump made her a horse everyone remembers!

MARION COAKES

Although Marion learned to ride on a donkey, when she was 13 she got her own pony, Stroller – who she'd eventually go to the Olympics with! As well as winning an individual silver medal at the 1968 Olympics, she won gold at the ladies' World Championship in 1965 and won three Nation's Cup events.

Most famous horse: Stroller

At only 14.2hh, Stroller was never expected to win at top-level competitions. However, Marion and Stroller were an unstoppable combination, taking home silver at the 1968 Olympics and beating the world's best horses!

JOHN WHITAKER

John Whitaker needs no introduction – he's been winning showjumping championships for Great Britain for more than 30 years. He's won 24 European, World and Olympic medals and is still competing today at the age of 62!

Most famous horse: Milton

Possibly the most famous showjumper ever, Milton had won more than £1.25m in prize money by the time he retired in 1994.

BEN MAHER

Ben began building up a winning reputation from a young age – he was ranked number one in Britain and number five in the world at just 26.

Most famous moment...

Helping Team GB to victory in the London 2012 Olympics – the first showjumping gold medal for Britain in 60 years!

PETER CHARLES

Peter Charles has competed on both the British and Irish teams at top level. In 1995, he won gold at the European Championships and was on the winning team for three Nation's Cup competitions.

Most famous moment...

Peter was the last to jump for Team GB at the London 2012 Olympics, but held his nerve to ride a brilliant clear round and secure the gold medal!

SCOTT BRASH

Scott Brash was the first ever rider to win showjumping's Grand Slam, by winning the three most prestigious events consecutively in 2015. He took home one million euros for his efforts!

Most famous horse: Hello Sanctos

Scott piloted Hello Sanctos to help win team gold in the 2012 Olympics, and together they've won countless more trophies, including The Global Champions Tour in 2013 and 2014.

THE UGLY DUCKLING

When Hannah fell off her dream pony, she thought she'd never ride again. Could Blue change her mind?

There's always that one pony at the riding school, isn't there? The one who no one wants to ride. Maybe he's lazy, maybe he bites when you do his girth up, or maybe he's just a bit ugly. This is a story about that pony at my riding school, and how he came to be my best friend.

My dream pony

Last year, I was the top rider at my riding school. Although my parents couldn't afford a pony, I shared a beautiful dun called Cookie. I trusted him to do anything – we went to showjumping competitions and had even jumped round our first British Showjumping affiliated course. We were unstoppable!

I thought there was nothing that could get between me and Cookie. He whinnied when I arrived on my share days and I made the most of every minute I had with him. That is, until the unthinkable happened.

The accident

A new girl had arrived at the riding school that summer. She didn't have her own pony, but seemed to get all the ponies going beautifully, no matter what tricks they got up to. She soon moved up the ranks in lessons until we were often sharing jumping lessons with our instructor, Karen.

"A flawless clear round, Susie!" Karen praised the new girl as she finished a foot-perfect course. She was riding a pony who, up until recently, had always knocked down poles. None of us knew how she managed it."Your turn to jump, Hannah."

I gathered up my reins in a hurry – I'd got distracted watching Susie ride and hadn't given Cookie a chance to get focused again. But I didn't want to give Karen a reason to think Susie was a better rider than me, so I gave Cookie a quick tap with my whip to wake him up and popped into canter, looking at the first fence in the course.

"Three, two, one," I counted down in my head as we approached the upright. It was a simple, inviting fence, so I wasn't worried. Suddenly, Cookie screeched to a halt and I went flying over his neck and crashed into the wing.

After the fall

Everything that happened after the accident is still a bit of a blur to me. I remember Mum taking me to hospital to have my arm X-rayed. She breathed a sigh of relief when we were told nothing was broken – my wrist was just sprained. But I still had to have a couple of weeks off riding to give it time to heal properly.

> "Tearfully, I agreed it was best to stop sharing Cookie until my confidence came back"

"Don't worry, Hannah," Mum tried to reassure me, "it won't be long until you're back in the saddle." I gulped and tried to fake a smile for her. I couldn't think of anything worse than riding again – let alone jumping – but I didn't want Mum to be disappointed in me, so I kept my nerves a secret.

The two weeks passed quickly and my arm felt stronger with each day. When it was time to return to the stables, I felt panic flood through me. I just had to let Mum know what was going on.

After explaining everything, she understood. We chatted for what felt like hours about the best thing to do. Tearfully, I agreed it was best to stop sharing Cookie until my confidence came back. He was such a talented pony, it was only fair for another girl from the riding school to have a chance with him.

We headed to the yard to tell Karen our decision and see if there were any other ponies I could have a lesson on. I still wasn't sure whether I was ready to get back on board, but I knew I wanted to give Cookie one last proper cuddle, at least.

Meeting Blue

Karen nodded kindly as I told her my decision about Cookie. "Don't worry," she said, "he'll get lots of love and attention with a new rider, and you'll still be able to see him all the time!" She paused, thoughtfully, "I've already got the perfect pony in mind for your first lesson back – Blue!"

My jaw dropped. "Blue?" I repeated in disbelief. "The Blue who no one likes to ride, who not even Susie can get to go forward?" Blue had been at the riding school longer than anyone could remember and no one wanted to be down to ride him in lessons. He was normally used for total beginners, as he didn't do much other than walk.

"Come and meet him," Karen persuaded me, "You'll be surprised. He's just a bit of an ugly duckling." I'd never given Blue a second look, but I agreed to meet him at least.

As I reached his stable, I was greeted by the sight of his scruffy tail. As usual, his head was in the back corner of the stable munching on his hay. Rather nervously, I went in.

"Hi, Blue," I murmured as I walked up to him, scratching his withers. He looked up from his hay and blew into my face. I giggled as his whiskers tickled against my cheek and he pushed his face towards my chest, asking to be stroked. I wondered why I'd never stopped to stroke him before. I suppose I'd always been put off by the sight of him trailing along in a lead-rein lesson.

Karen led him out of the stable for me and helped me tack up. I gulped as I put my foot in the stirrup to get on. Was I ready for this?

Back in the saddle

I couldn't have predicted how well that first lesson went. I had been so nervous, but Blue looked after me every step of the way. We spent the whole lesson in walk and only built up to trot and canter over the next couple of weeks when I felt ready.

It was almost as if we both needed each other. Stuck with the beginner riders, Blue hadn't had a chance to show his true potential – he'd grown so used to the kicking and pulling, and had kept plodding on as he thought best.

After a few months, I took Blue on full loan. I spent all my spare time with him. As soon as the bell rang at end of school, I was out the door and on my way to the yard. Before long, we even started jumping again and moved our way back up the group lessons.

It was bound to happen, but I was still shocked when I was placed in a group lesson with Susie, who was riding Cookie. She looked Blue up and down as she rode past and shook her head. "Oh dear," she said, "I didn't know Blue could even jump." I decided not to get annoyed by her comments. "Cookie looks great," I smiled back at her, "you must be doing really well with him." Susie rolled her eyes and trotted off to warm up.

I was determined not to let Susie get to me this time. I couldn't let anything distract me. All that mattered was me and Blue.

Success!

The lesson couldn't have gone any better. Blue went perfectly for me and as we landed over the final fence in the course, I felt a weight lift from my shoulders. We could do it, after all!

Although I didn't know it at the time, Blue was the answer to all my problems. I genuinely thought I'd never want to ride again after my accident, but Blue helped me like no other pony could. We've even started competing now, and we won our first red rosette not too long ago. He's definitely the best pony in the world, and I couldn't imagine riding any other pony but him.

QUIZ!

What colour's that?

Do you know your bays from your greys and your stars from your stripes? Take our quiz to test your knowledge of horsey colours and markings!

MATCH THE MARKINGS

1. Match the face marking to the correct picture...

- **A** star
- **B** stripe
- **C** blaze
- **D** snip

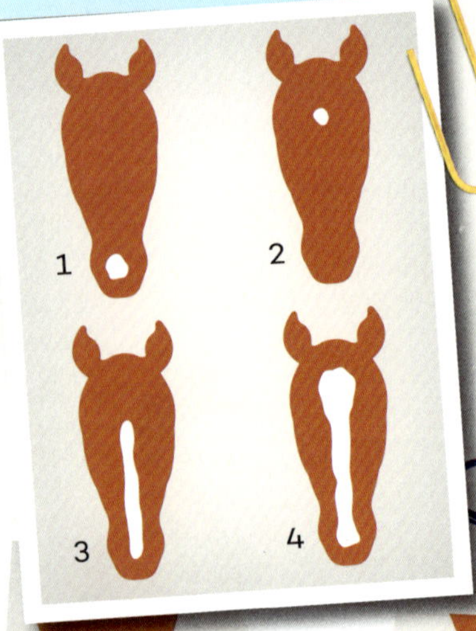

2. Now match the leg markings...

- **A** sock
- **B** stocking
- **C** coronet
- **D** ermine marks

CORRECT COLOURS

3. Can you correctly identify the colour of these horses?

A

B

C

D

4. What about these horses? Careful, these are a bit more tricky...

A

B

C

D

THE LIGHTNING ROUND

5. What's the name for a pony's blue eye?

6. What's the name of the dark line that runs along the spine of a dun pony?

7. Blue and strawberry are both types of which pony colour?

8. Haflingers are palomino – true or false?

9. Skewbald ponies are white with patches of any colour other than black – true or false?

10. Grey ponies have been that colour their whole life – true or false?

11. Liver is a shade of which colour?

12. What's the name for a place where coat growing in different directions meets?

Turn to page 100 to find out how you got on!

Dressage LEGENDS

Dressage is a test of obedience, with horses and riders performing impressive movements seamlessly. Find out about the legends of the sport!

CHARLOTTE DUJARDIN

Charlotte is currently one of the best-known names in the dressage world! Carl Hester gave her the ride on the then-undiscovered Valegro, and the pair went on to win every major competition in the world!

Most famous horse: Valegro

This world record-beating horse has a huge medal haul to his name, winning individual gold and team silver at the 2016 Rio Olympics and individual and team gold at London 2012, as well as countless other European and World Championship medals. The pair currently hold the world record scores in all top-level tests!

LEE PEARSON

Lee has been riding for the British para-dressage team since 1999 and has won 30 gold medals at para-dressage European and World Championships, and at the Paralympics.

Most famous achievement...

Lee set the record for being unbeaten at three consecutive Paralympic games, winning the team, individual and freestyle gold medals in 2000, 2004 and 2008.

EDWARD GAL

Edward rides for The Netherlands, and has won a total of six gold medals at World and European Championship levels.

Most famous horse: Moorlands Totilas

Edward and Totilas wowed the crowds at the 2010 World Equestrian Games, being the first combination to ever win all three gold medals on offer!

SOPHIE CHRISTIANSEN

Sophie has competed in four Paralympic Games for the British team and she's won a seriously impressive 10 Paralympic medals! At her first Paralympics, in Athens in 2004, she was the youngest rider competing, aged only 16.

Most famous achievement...

Winning two individual and one team gold Olympic medals for a second time at the 2016 Rio Olympics – repeating her successes from the 2012 London Olympics.

LAURA TOMLINSON

Laura is a British rider who's won two Olympic medals – both at the 2012 London Olympics. She won three silver medals at the 2010 World Equestrian Games, as well as team gold and individual bronze at the 2011 European Championships.

Most famous achievement...

Laura was part of the gold medal-winning team at London 2012 and also took home individual bronze.

CARL HESTER

Carl is a familiar face on the British Dressage team, having competed in four Olympic games. He holds nine senior championship medals, and has also won a staggering 63 national championship titles!

Most famous horse: Uthopia

Carl and Uthopia won two individual silvers and a team gold at the 2011 European Championships. At the 2012 London Olympics, they helped the British team secure its first ever dressage Olympic medal – a gold!

ANKY VAN GRUNSVEN

Anky is a dressage rider from The Netherlands, and is the only rider to have competed at every single World Equestrian Games since they began in 1990. She's won nine Olympic medals, and holds many more from World and European Championships.

Most famous achievement...

Anky remains the only person to have competed at seven Olympic Games back-to-back and won three gold medals at three successive games – 2000, 2004 and 2008.

OFF THE BEATEN TRACK

Check out these different types of hacking and find out why they're all so great!

FIND FREEDOM IN THE FIELDS

The fields at your yard are a great introduction to hacking if you've only ridden in an arena before. Some farmers leave set-asides around the edges of their field for you to ride on, too.

Best bits include...

- if you're a little nervous, fields are more enclosed than most other types of hacking
- riding through longer grass will make your pony really lift his legs, which is a great workout

Watch out for...

- rabbit holes and uneven ground – they might be hidden under long grass
- fields that are used for crops – never ride on these
- always check with the land owner that you have permission to ride in their fields

"Fields at your yard are a great introduction if you've only ridden in an arena before"

Fun factor
2/5

THE OPEN ROAD

You might think riding on the road is boring, or even dangerous, but it's important your pony's used to hacking on them because there aren't many places you can get to without at least a little bit of roadwork.

Best bits include...

- your pony will get used to different environments and learn to adapt to new, busy places more quickly
- occasionally riding on a hard surface is a good change for your pony
- roads can lead you to so much more!

Watch out for...

- traffic – especially buses, lorries, tractors and fast cars
- blind bends – you can't always see what's coming and other road users might not see you coming, either
- slippy tarmac and drains – if your pony wears shoes, avoid stepping on these hazards

Fun factor 1/5

HIT THE BEACH

There's nowhere better to go for a gallop or a stroll, whatever you prefer. The beach is deffo one of the most exciting places to ride, ever!

Best bits include...

- you can relax and enjoy the change of scenery
- there's plenty of space to race your mates
- your pony will love the soft ground
- having a paddle in the sea

Watch out for...

- other beach users – they might not be expecting a pony to come charging past, so be careful
- big waves – your pony won't appreciate a soggy face, so stick to the shallows
- tide times – you'll have the most space at low tide and you don't want to get caught out at high tide, so check the tide times before you set off
- your pony rolling – some ponies like to have a cheeky roll in the sea, so stay alert!

Fun factor 5/5

GO WILD IN THE WOODS

Riding in the woods is super-fun, especially if you love to jump. And there are normally lots of routes, so every time you go you can do something a little different.

Best bits include...

- logs and branches to jump
- weaving between trees can keep your pony really interested
- shade in the heat of summer
- the tree covering means the ground takes longer to dry out, so sometimes when everywhere else is too hard, you can still find somewhere to go for a canter

Watch out for...

- tree roots – if you and your pony aren't concentrating he could easily trip
- other riders appearing from what seems like nowhere – woods are popular, so keep your eyes peeled
- dodgy take-off and landing areas. Always check these before you jump

TOP HACKING TIPS

- **Always tell an adult where you're going and how long for**
- **Go with a friend so that you can look out for each other**
- **Always wear high-vis if you're riding on the road**
- **Take a fully charged phone with you**

EXPLORE THE TRACKS

Networks of tracks and bridleways are a mega-handy way of getting from A to B and skipping some roadwork, and they're fun, too.

Best bits include...

- you're off-road, so there's no need to worry about traffic
- the ground is normally quite varied, which is great for your pony

Watch out for...

- low branches – practise your ducking position before you go
- walkers – pedestrians and cyclists are allowed on bridleways, too

Fun factor 3/5

"Tracks and bridleways are a mega-handy way of getting from A to B, and they're fun, too"

BIG UP THE OPEN SPACES

If you have access to a heath or common, there are so many ways you can make the most of this extra space.

Best bits include...

- you can practise your dressage test or individual show in a different place
- you can use the extra space to stretch your pony's legs (at speed!)

Watch out for...

- livestock – often commons are used for grazing cattle, sheep or ponies. You can still ride there, but take extra care
- getting too fast – in such an open space it's even more important that you're always in control of your pony
- dogs – heaths and commons are really popular with dog walkers. Ask owners politely to put their dog on a lead if they aren't already

Fun factor 4/5

BEST OF BRITISH BREEDS WELSH

Venture west and meet the pretty and popular Welsh pony!

FAST FACTS

Height: From under 12hh to over 13.2hh, depending on type. Section Ds can be up to 16hh

Colour: Any solid colour. Markings are allowed but piebalds, skewbalds and spotted coats aren't

Place of origin: Wales

The pony for you if... you want a versatile pony with lots of personality and seriously good looks!

The Welsh pony breed is actually made up of four different types, each with distinctive features and purposes. These types, or sections, have been developed over the breed's long history, creating hardy ponies who can turn a hoof to any job they're needed for!

DID YOU KNOW?

Welsh ponies and cobs are known for being good-doers – this is because in the wild, food is scarce and requires them to cross treacherous terrain.

Spoilt for choice

The Welsh breed has a type to suit every rider, so you're sure to find something you like! Each section shares a few distinctive characteristics – a pretty dished face, long, arched neck, and strong, muscular body.

- **The Welsh Mountain Pony, or Section A**, is the smallest of the types, and must not exceed 12hh. Section As have been referred to as the prettiest breed of pony in the world – and it's not hard to see why, with their flowing manes and tails, delicate, dished faces, and large, long-lashed eyes! Clever and kind, they make great first ponies and excel in showing, jumping and gymkhana games.
- **The Welsh Pony, or Section B**, is a slightly larger riding pony, ranging from 12hh to 13.2hh. The Section B is similar in type to the Section A, but with a longer neck and legs, and a more animated trot. They make versatile all-rounders and can excel in all disciplines. With their sweet, spirited nature, they're a popular choice.
- **The Welsh Pony of Cob Type, or Section C**, can range from 12hh to 13.2hh but is heavier-set than the Section B, so they can carry a larger rider. Section Cs are talented jumpers and are very sure footed, so they make fab hacking partners.
- **The Welsh Cob, or Section D**, must be over 13.2hh, and is a refined, athletic cob type. Famous for their stamina and expressive gaits, Section Ds are a firm favourite for children and adults, and can be spotted dominating international driving competitions!

DID YOU KNOW?
In the early 1900s, Welsh ponies were only accepted into the studbook if they could trot 35 miles uphill from Cardiff to Dowlais without stopping. The test took three hours to complete – so it's no surprise that nowadays, they're often used for endurance!

Not just a pretty face

Descended from Celtic ponies who roamed the wild Welsh countryside in prehistoric times, the Welsh breed has been carefully developed over the last 2,000 years. Initially prized by farmers for their hardiness and ability to cross tricky terrain, they became invaluable to the efforts of coal miners, who used them to pull coal carts in and out of the mines. Small, tough ponies were invaluable for this job, as it required them to work deep underground in seriously small tunnels.

It's thought that Arab blood was first introduced to the breed in the Middle Ages, when knights returned from the Middle East with Arab stallions that they'd captured in battle. In the 1700s, Hackney and Norfolk Roadster blood was added to create the distinctive movement that the ponies still have today.

Practical ponies

Modern Welsh ponies and cobs are more likely to be found in the show ring than in the coal mines – the breed does brilliantly in show pony, riding pony, cob, and mountain and moorland classes from local level through to the big leagues at the Horse of the Year Show. They're also a great choice for Pony Clubbers, as they can turn a hoof to any discipline and with such big personalities they can teach their riders loads!

DID YOU KNOW?
A small, semi-feral herd of just under 200 ponies still roams the Carneddau mountains in Wales.

The Welsh breed comes from Wales, and has close ties to the Carneddau mountains in Snowdonia. These are the largest areas of high ground in Wales and England!

QUIZ!

What does that mean?

The horse world has its own language and it's easy to get confused. Test your knowledge of horsey words with this quiz!

PARTS OF THE HORSE

Use the clues to unscramble the names of different parts of your pony's body

1. SKINAG
The muscular area of your pony's hindleg between his stifle and hock.

2. SHEWRIT
The ridge at the base of your pony's neck – the point where he's measured from.

3. RENTASP
The part of the leg between your pony's fetlock and hoof.

4. CUPOR
The highest point of your pony's hindquarters.

5. SHENTUCT
A round, horny growth on the inside of your pony's leg.

BREEDS OF HORSE

We've removed the vowels and spacing from these breeds of horse from all over the world. Can you figure out which ones they are?

6. HNVRN
7. CLYDDL
8. CLNDC
9. RSHDRGHT
10. KHLTK

WEIRD WORDS

Can you pick the correct definition of these horsey words?

11. What's piaffe?

- A A dressage movement
- B A grooming spray that adds volume to your pony's mane
- C A tasty pony treat

12. What's a grackle?

- A A poisonous plant
- B A type of noseband
- C Another name for a hacking jacket

13. Which is these is not vaulting?

- A A sport that involves gymnastics on horseback
- B When knights charge at each other with lances
- C Mounting your pony by leaping onto his back

14. Which of these is not a Trakehner?

- A A type of bit
- B A cross-country fence
- C A breed of horse

15. What's another name for an arena?

- A Ménege
- B Minage
- C Manège

Turn to page 100 to check your answers!

Make

FRIENDSHIP BRACELETS!

You'll need...
- ✓ coloured string
- ✓ beads
- ✓ sticky tape
- ✓ scissors

Make matching friendship bracelets for you and your yard mates!

TO MAKE A PLAITED BRACELET...

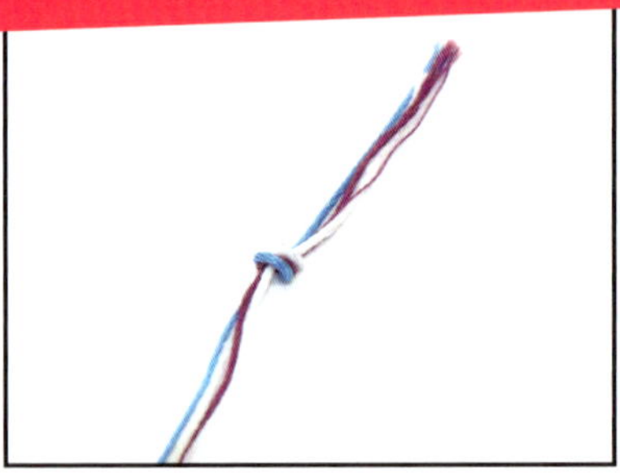

1. Choose three colours of string about 20cm long and tie a knot 3–4cm from the top.

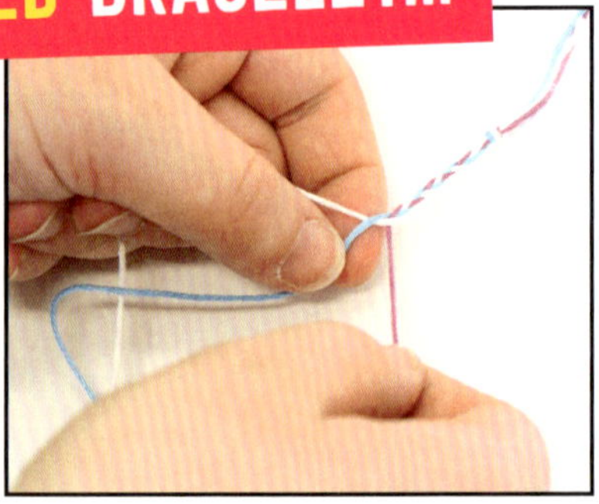

2. Plait the threads until the bracelet is long enough to wrap around your wrist.

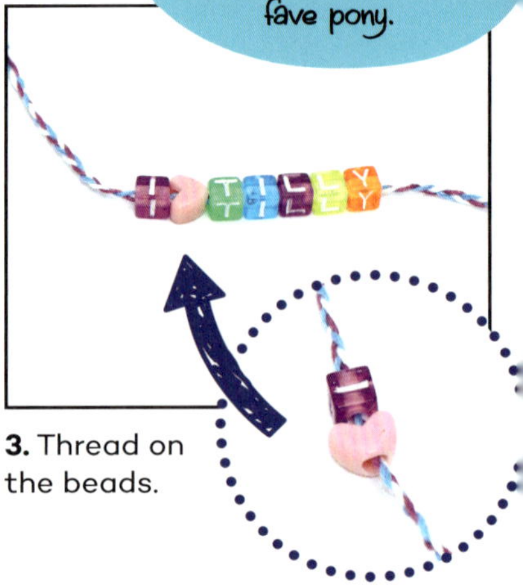

3. Thread on the beads.

TOP TIP Use lettered beads to write the name of your friend's fave pony.

4. Tie a quick-release knot at the end to create a loop. Secure it with another knot around it.

5. Cut the spare thread. Your bracelet is ready to tie – secure the loose end to the loop.

TOP TIP If you want to make a thicker plait, use six threads (two of each colour). Make sure this will fit through your beads first, though.

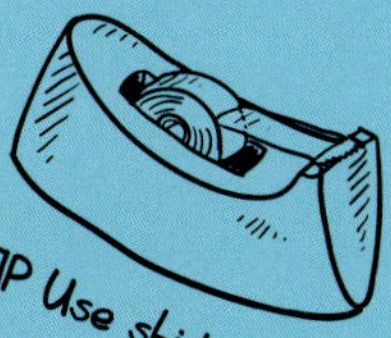

TO MAKE A KNOTTED BRACELET...

TOP TIP Use sticky tape to attach the thread to a table so it doesn't move while you're plaiting.

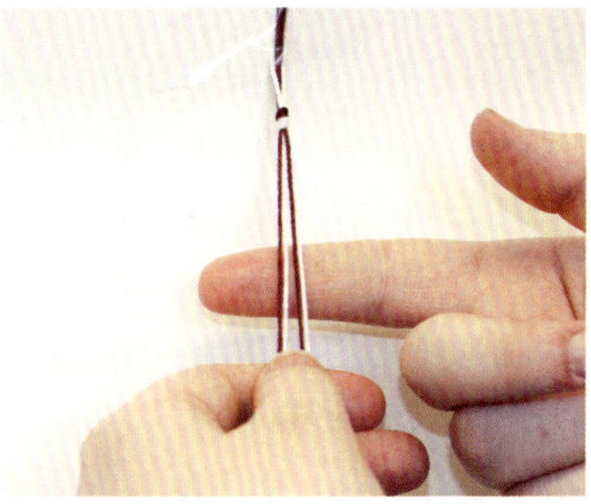

1. Using two colours, cut four threads about 40cm long. Tie a knot about 3cm from the top.

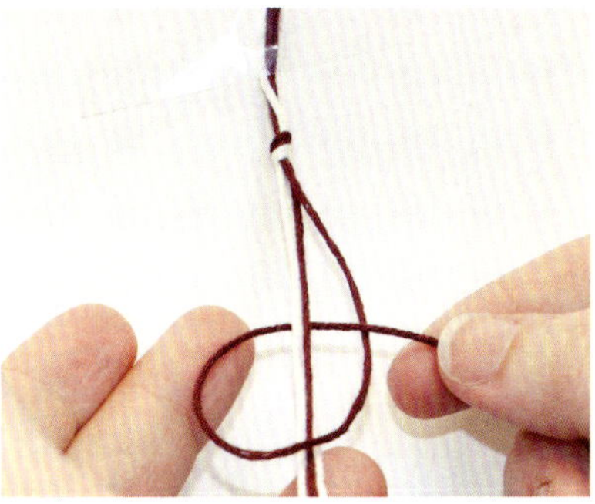

2. Take one thread and wrap it over and around the other three, pulling it through the loop you've made as if you're tying a knot.

3. Pull the knot tight, pushing it up to the top as you do.

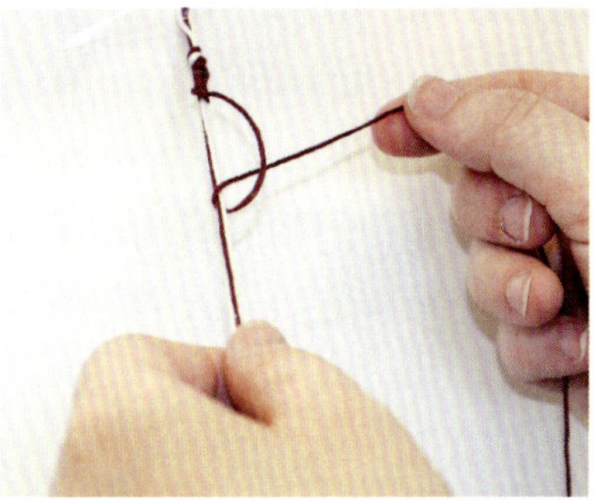

4. Repeat steps 2 and 3 with the same thread until you've made 12 knots.

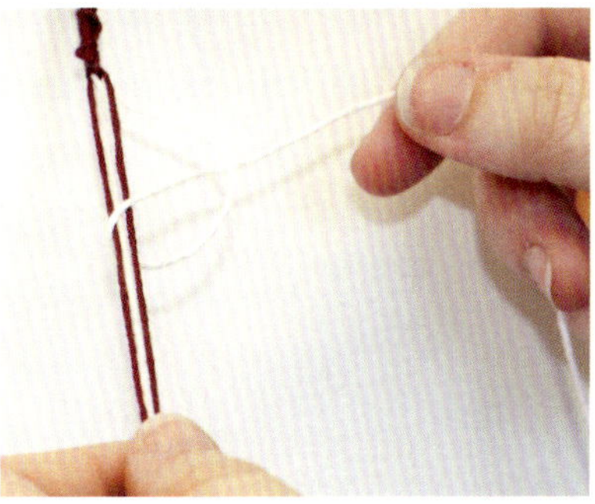

5. Take a thread in the other colour and repeat steps 2 and 3 until you've made 12 more knots.

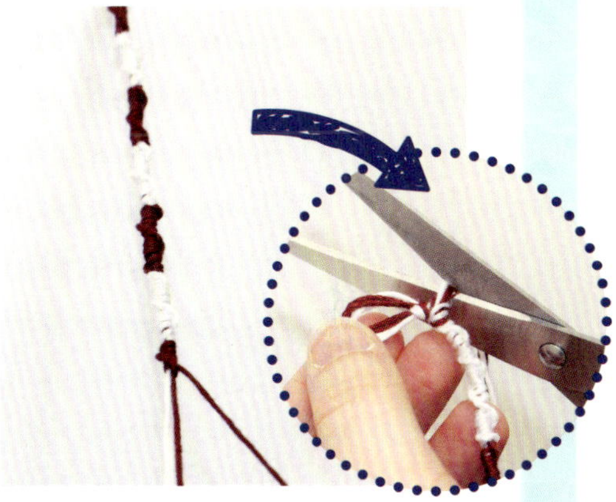

6. Keep swapping colour every 12 knots until the bracelet is long enough to tie around your wrist.

7. Finish it off in the same way as steps 4 and 5 of the plaited bracelet.

TOP TIP Use your friends' cross-country colours to make the bracelets extra-special.

BFFs

TA-DAH!

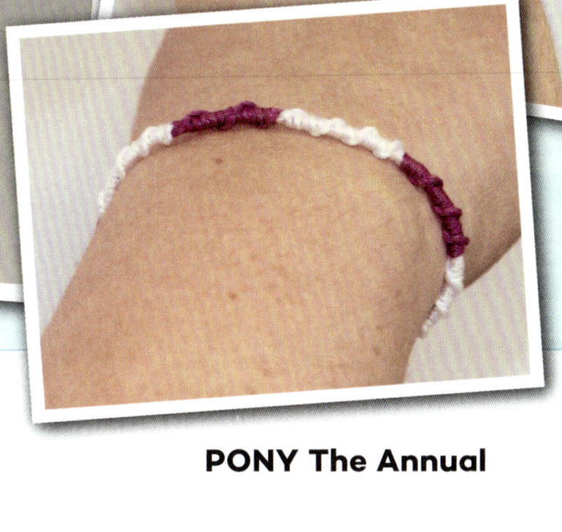

QUIZ!

What's your dream horsey job?

Do you want a job that revolves around horses? Take our quiz to find out which one is right for you

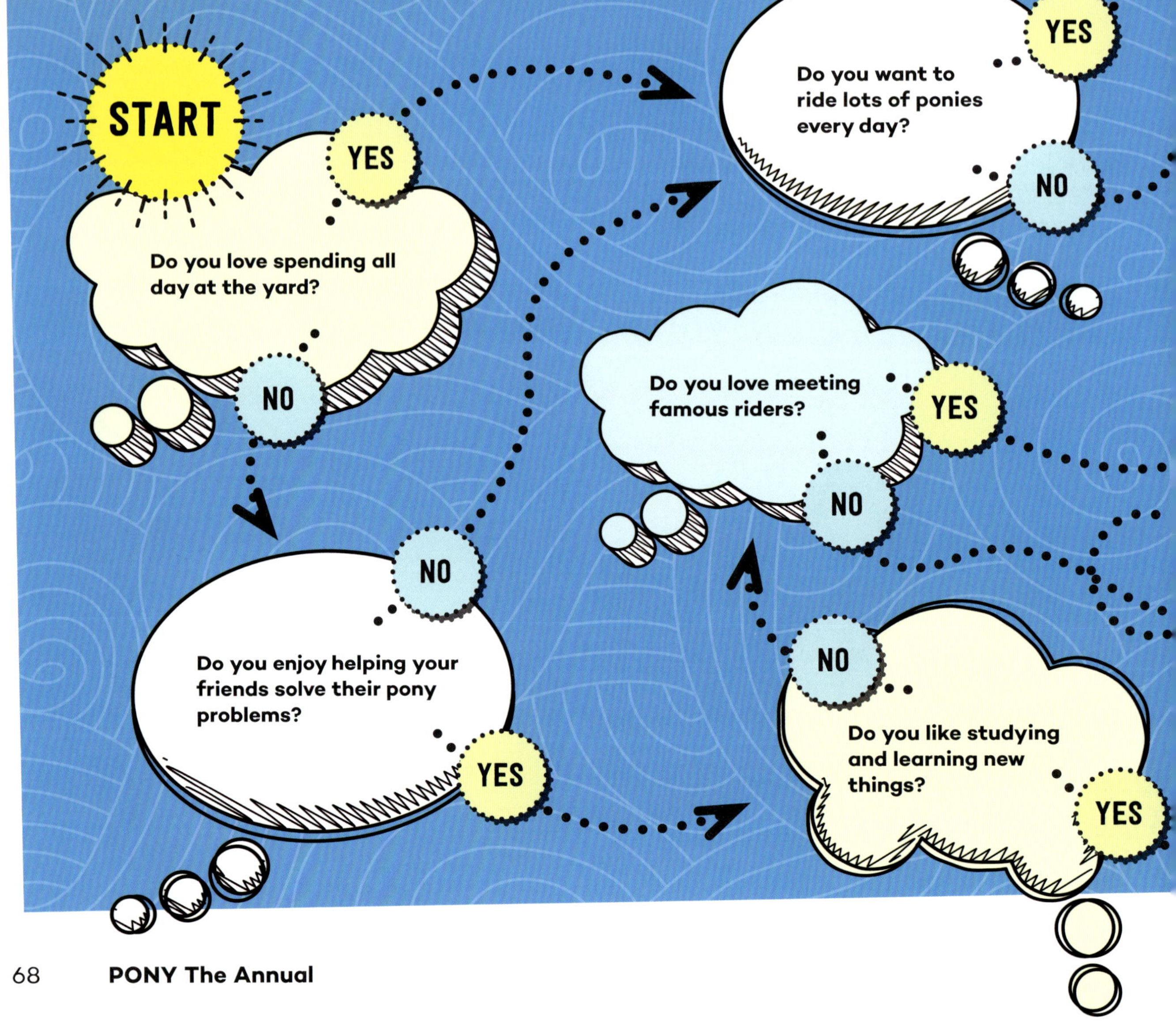

Is going to a big show such as Badminton or Olympia the best day out ever?

YES → Are you super-competitive?

NO → Do you really want to work with ponies in need?

Are you super-competitive?

YES → Professional Rider

NO → Equestrian Journalist

Do you really want to work with ponies in need?

YES → Horsey Charity Worker

NO → Equestrian Journalist

Are you really interested in anatomy and how your pony moves?

YES → Physiotherapist

NO → Horsey Charity Worker

PROFESSIONAL RIDER

Your perfect job involves riding horses all day long – amazing! Whatever your chosen discipline, if you work hard and dream big, it could be you riding at Olympia or Badminton in the future!

EQUESTRIAN JOURNALIST

Would being on Team PONY be the coolest thing ever?! If you dream of interviewing celeb riders, going on photoshoots and helping readers learn more about caring for their ponies, then being a equestrian journalist is the job for you.

HORSEY CHARITY WORKER

There are loads of different jobs you can do for a horsey charity, from looking after the super-cute ponies at a rescue centre to organising fundraising activities. The most important thing is that you're passionate about helping ponies in need.

PHYSIOTHERAPIST

If you like meeting people and their ponies, you'll love being a physiotherapist. It's a key part in helping ponies stay sound and performing at their best, from leisure ponies all the way through to top athletes, so it's a very important job.

HORSE SPORTS

SIDE SADDLE

Side saddle is the traditional way ladies used to ride horses, but it still exists today. Find out all about it!

Side saddle riding dates back thousands of years, with the first images being seen on Ancient Greek vases. The type of side saddle that's used today dates all the way back to the 1830s, and gives you the security in the saddle to be able to gallop and jump.

At the time, it was thought improper for women to ride astride, and the long dresses and skirts they wore meant that it was easier to ride aside. Although times have changed, side saddle riding still takes place, often in the show ring and sometimes even on the hunting field!

Saddle up!

Unlike a normal saddle, there are two pommels on a side saddle. Your right leg goes over the top pommel and hangs down, while your left leg sits under the second pommel, and a stirrup is used as normal on this side.

Your legs should stay relaxed and soft on the saddle, but if you get into a sticky situation, you can grip the two pommels for extra security!

DID YOU KNOW?

A traditional side saddle is, on average, around 6kg heavier than a normal saddle.

PONY magazine recommends you wear an up-to-standard riding hat at all times when mounted

DID YOU KNOW?

In 2013, Irish rider Susan Oakes set a new side saddle high jump world record – clearing a whopping 2.03m on her horse, SIEC Atlas!

On the straight and narrow

Despite the name, when riding side saddle, your body should be completely straight. From behind, it should look the same as if you were riding astride from the waist up. Any twisting in your body, hands or legs can put extra pressure on one side of your pony – this is one of the first things judges look for in a showing class.

Riders often wear a spur on their left leg and always hold a whip in their right hand to work as the leg aid.

DID YOU KNOW?

Modern side saddles are difficult to come by, and expensive. Most riders use old side saddles, but these often need a lot of work to make sure they fit both horse and rider.

What to wear

The traditional clothes worn by a side saddle rider are known as a habit, made up of a jacket and a matching apron. The apron is an open-back skirt that covers the legs, allowing jodhpurs to be worn underneath. When riders dismount, the apron can be wrapped behind their legs and buttoned up to look like a skirt.

Showing off

There are loads of different types of showing classes dedicated to side saddle riders. These include equitation classes where the rider is judged, concours d'élégance classes where the overall picture of horse and rider is judged, and normal type classes such as mountain and moorland, working hunter and coloureds. There are even dressage and showjumping classes!

For those who like a real challenge, some side saddle riders even take up steeplechase races and team chasing, where riders gallop miles across country, jumping huge hedges and natural fences!

Boost YOUR CONFIDENCE!

No confidence crisis here! Find out how to build your confidence around ponies, whether it's on the ground or in the saddle

Every pony has his own personality – and that's why we love them! But this can mean they're unpredictable, which is nerve-racking if you don't feel totally confident. If any of these problems sound like your confidence hang-ups, read on to find out how to tackle them head-on.

Handling confidence

"I'm not sure how to do it!"
If you're not quite sure how to do something – whether it's catching, tacking up or picking out hooves – ask! It's hard to be confident if you're unsure and, worse, it can cause an accident.

Ask your instructor or someone experienced to walk you through how to do it and help you practise. There's nothing wrong with asking for a helping hand, and the more you know about handling ponies on the ground, the more comfortable you'll feel completing everyday tasks. Once you know that you can do it properly, your confidence will grow.

"I haven't done it before"

Remember – practice makes perfect. No one gets everything absolutely right from the beginning and the best way to learn is by doing it yourself.

There are lots of things to remember when you're handling ponies on the ground, so ask someone experienced to help the first few times, and then give it a go on your own. It's best to practise on a sensible pony to begin with, so he won't get irritated if things take a bit longer than usual.

TOP TIP

If you're not confident handling your pony, remember to keep breathing! Ponies can sense nervous behaviour, which often makes them feel nervous, too. The more confident you seem on the outside, the more relaxed your pony will feel!

TOP TIP

Dress for the job! Make sure you're wearing boots, gloves and a riding hat when you're handling a pony. It'll help you feel more confident to know you're in the correct safety gear.

TOP TIP

Don't be afraid to speak up if you're not comfortable handling a pony in a certain situation. It's better for someone to help you and give you confidence than for something to go wrong.

TOP TIP

Take the time to bond with the pony you're handling. Give him a scratch on his neck and talk to him. The more you trust each other, the more confident you'll feel.

"I don't know this pony!"

You might be super-confident handling your fave pony – you know all his quirks and how he reacts in different situations. But it's normal to be more apprehensive handling a new pony, so don't worry.

Ask his owner if there's anything you need to know about him, first. He might be sensitive when you do up his girth, or always spook in the same place when you turn him out. Knowing these things in advance will let you prepare for them, so you can avoid any situations you might be unsure about.

> "It's normal to be more apprehensive handling a strange pony, so don't worry"

Riding confidence

"I don't like people watching me"

It's really common to feel under pressure and nervous if there are people watching while you're riding. Whether you're at a competition or schooling, it can be hard to concentrate if you're worried about what people are thinking.

Try to stay focused on what you're doing with your pony, ride to the best of your abilities, and block everything else from your mind. Practise getting used to it by asking your friends to come and watch while you're schooling – you'll soon forget they're there!

"I might fall off!"

It's never nice falling off and it's something all riders try to avoid. It's common to be nervous about it, but if you get too worried it'll cause you to tense up while you're riding – making it more likely for you to fall off!

If you're worrying about it, give your shoulders a wriggle and try to relax in the saddle. Take a deep breath and smile – if you look confident on the outside, you'll feel more confidence on the inside.

TOP TIP

If you've had a confidence knock, think about asking to ride a calm, experienced pony for a while. It'll help you get your confidence back up again in no time at all.

"That fence looks huge!"

Lots of riders feel nervous jumping, especially if they're tackling fences bigger than usual. But remember, your instructor wouldn't ask you to jump something if they didn't think you and your pony were capable of it. Sit up, look ahead, and kick on.

If you've had a real knock to your confidence, don't be afraid to go back to basics. There's nothing wrong with starting small and building your way back up again.

"I might lose control"
Ponies are big animals and much stronger than us, too. If you're worried about losing control and your pony running off with you, try to stay positive. If you know you can control your pony in the school, there's no reason you can't when you're in a field or on a hack.

Use half-halts to keep him focused on you, but don't keep pulling on the reins – if you pull, he'll find it uncomfortable and pull back, making you both more stressed!

> "Use half-halts to keep your pony focused on you"

TOP TIP

Remember, the more time you spend in the saddle, the more confident you'll feel. Confidence doesn't grow overnight, so keep working hard and practising – you'll get there eventually!

The new ARRIVAL

Ella's cousin is moving to her yard, but is it going to be fun and problem-free?

Katie and Hunter
as **Ella and Freddie**

Charlotte and Cloud
as **Zoe and Alfie**

Ellie and Rabbit
as **Claire and Lottie**

THE NEXT DAY...
Come on, Freddie, where do you want to go today?
Have you seen Ella? Do you know what time she's getting here?
No, I thought you'd text her.
I thought you were going with Claire?
Hey, where have you been? We thought you were coming with us?
Nooo, we spent all day planning where we'd go together. Zoe told me you know the best routes.
Yeah, sorry, I just forgot to text you. Totally my bad!

I KNEW IT!
This is so awkward, Freddie, we'd better leave before they see us!
I hope she doesn't think we're going without her!
Oh dear, let's call her to check.
NO ANSWER.
You didn't go far did you, Ella? Why don't we all go for a ride now?
Okay! I should have just asked you what your plans were, rather than assuming the worst.
Shall we go for another ride again tomorrow?
YES!
Well I'm glad that's sorted, there are so many rides I want you to show us!
The end

QUIZ!

What's the problem?

Would you know if your pony wasn't feeling quite right? Take our quiz to find out whether you're super at spotting his symptoms

PROBLEM 1

Your pony has developed a hard, bony lump on the inside of the cannon bone on his front leg. What could it be?

- **A** A bite
- **B** A splint
- **C** An injured tendon

PROBLEM 2

Matted areas of hair with crusty scabs have appeared on your pony's lower legs. When the scabs are lifted, the skin looks sore and has serum oozing from it. What could it be?

- **A** An allergic reaction
- **B** A kick wound
- **C** Mud fever

PROBLEM 3

Your pony has been scratching his mane and top of his tail on anything that's available. Now the hair is wearing away, and his skin looks sore and damaged. What could it be?

- **A** Sunburn
- **B** Sweet itch
- **C** Ringworm

PROBLEM 4

Your pony is standing strangely, looking like he's leaning back. He's reluctant to move and his front feet feel warm. What could it be?

- **A** Laminitis
- **B** A suspensory ligament injury
- **C** Arthritis

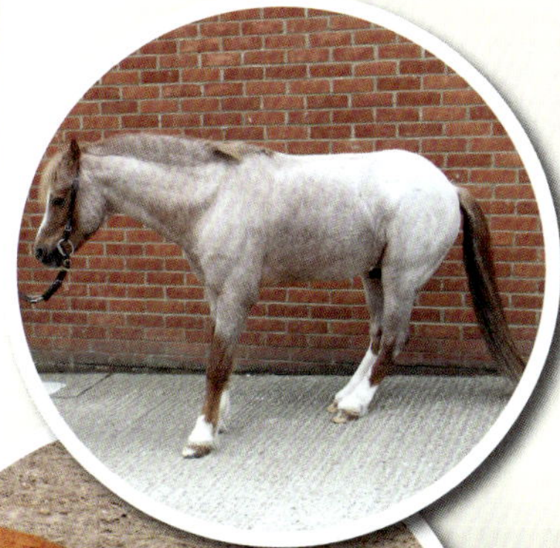

PROBLEM 5

Your pony looks uncomfortable, is pawing at the ground, getting up and down, looking at his tummy and rolling. It's been a while since he last did a poo, too. What could it be?

- **A** Gastric ulcers
- **B** Choke
- **C** Colic

PROBLEM 6

Your pony's coat has become really thick, long and curly, and he had trouble losing it when his coat changed in spring. He's lost weight and developed a pot belly, seems to sweat more, and has been drinking and weeing more than usual, too. What could it be?

- **A** Lice
- **B** PPID (Cushing's disease)
- **C** Rainscald

PROBLEM 7

When you return from a ride, you notice your pony has a wound on his front leg, on the bulb of his heel. It's a slice and is bleeding slightly. What could it be?

- **A** An overreach
- **B** Nail bind
- **C** Thrush

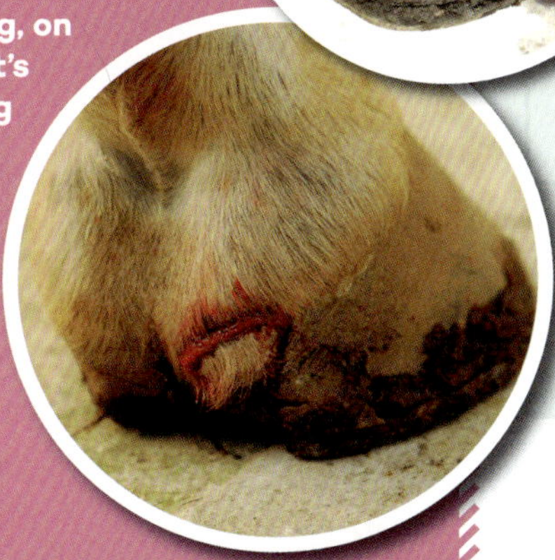

PROBLEM 8

Your pony has developed a small, knobbly lump on his skin that's hairless, crusty and ulcerated. What could it be?

- **A** A fly bite
- **B** Nettle rash
- **C** A sarcoid

PROBLEM 9

It's been a sunny week and your pony's pink nose has gone red, inflamed, cracked and crusty. What could it be?

- **A** Nettle rash
- **B** Sweet itch
- **C** Sunburn

PROBLEM 10

You pick out your pony's hoof and notice that it's smelly and there's some black discharge. His frog has gone a bit soft, too. What could it be?

- **A** Thrush
- **B** Nail bind
- **C** Navicular syndrome

Turn to page 100 to check your answers!

BEST OF BRITISH BREEDS

DARTMOOR

Head to the West Country and meet the dinky but delightful Dartmoor pony

The Dartmoor pony has roamed the moors of the West Country since the agricultural age around 3,500–5,500 years ago, proving its worth by being a great help to early farming civilisations. Known for being kind, reliable and easy to keep, these days they make fab family ponies. Despite being small, they can easily carry a light adult rider.

FAST FACTS

Height: 12.2hh and under
Colour: Most commonly bay, but can be any solid colour
Place of origin: Devon
The pony for you if... you want a four-legged friend that everyone in your family can enjoy

DID YOU KNOW?

Feral Dartmoor ponies are rounded up each year for an annual health check and to ensure that any new foals born are recorded. This is called a drift.

Made for moorland

The Dartmoor pony is a small, tough type that has adapted to survive the harsh weather and sparse vegetation of its native home. As a result, they tend to have strong, sturdy legs and hard, strong hooves. Their shoulders are sloped, giving them free, open movement, and they have thick, flowing manes and tails. The most common colour for a Dartmoor pony is mousey brown with a mealy muzzle and black points, similar to the Exmoor pony, but all solid colours can be found.

A slice of history

Dartmoor ponies have lived on the moors since at least 1,500BC – but some evidence suggests it may be as long ago as 3,500BC! By medieval times, they'd established themselves as a useful partner for the working communities on the moor, and were used to pull heavy loads from the tin mines scattered around Devon. After the mines were shut down, most of the remaining pit ponies were set free to roam the moors.

In the early 1900s, Dartmoor ponies were bred at the local prison and used to help the guards move prisoners – talk about a tough job! After World War II, the breed's numbers declined, but thanks to the hard work of the Dartmoor Pony Society, they stabilised. Now, although the Dartmoor pony has been granted rare breed status, it's going from strength to strength and is an important and protected part of the local landscape.

PIGGY PONIES

It's illegal to feed feral Dartmoor ponies, as it encourages them to approach moving cars looking for yummy snacks and spare ice cream cones, putting them at risk. So if you see wild ponies in the park, enjoy them from afar!

DID YOU KNOW?

To keep Dartmoor ponies safe from local traffic, park wardens have experimented with painting reflective, high-vis stripes along the ponies' sides. Funky!

From moor to manège

Because of their ultra-sweet personalities and sturdy conformation, Dartmoor ponies can turn their talents to a variety of jobs. They're a popular choice for the show ring, and can also be found doing the mega-important job of teaching young riders to go from riding on the lead rein to flying solo! They also make great happy hackers and can even jump and be driven, too.

DID YOU KNOW?

Although Dartmoor ponies look quite similar to the neighbouring Exmoor ponies, they're not actually related. Archaeologists have recently discovered that they evolved from two totally different ancient pony types!

SHAPE UP YOUR FLATWORK

Being able to ride accurate shapes is super-important and it'll help make your schooling much more interesting, too. Here's some inspo to get you started...

Riding round and round the edge of the arena is boring for you and your pony. It's important to keep things interesting by riding lots of shapes and changes of rein – it'll help keep him more supple, too. Here are some shapes you can ride to mix up your flatwork...

DID YOU KNOW?
You can ride most of these exercises in lots of different parts of the school.

20m circle

A 20m circle is the best size to begin with because you can use the fence and X to help you get the right shape and size.

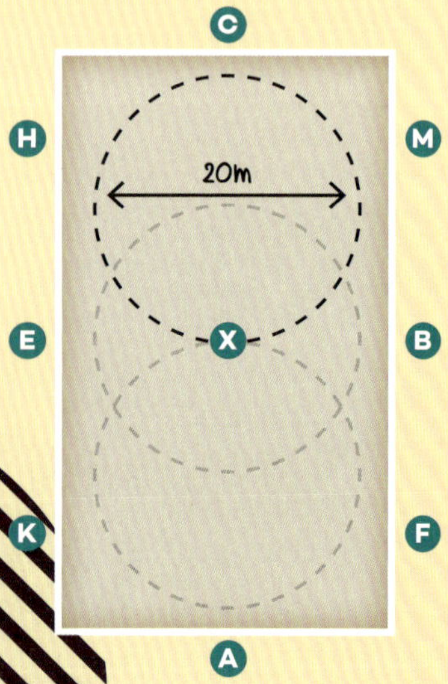

DID YOU KNOW?
It's called a 20m circle because the diameter is 20m. This is the measurement from one side of the circle to the other.

10m circle

It takes a little more balance because it's smaller, but you can ride 10m circles, too.

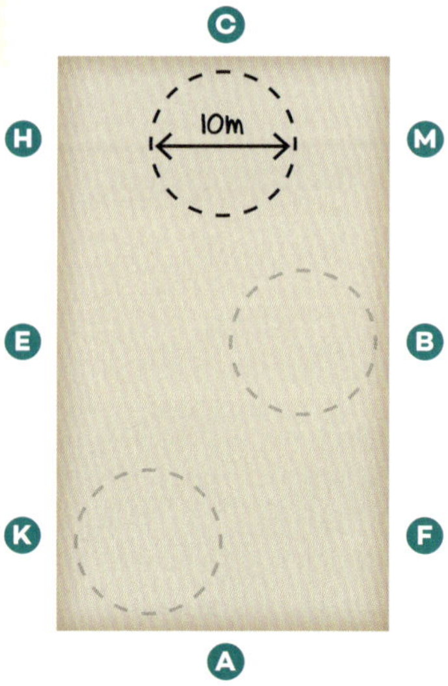

TOP TIP
Always look about ⅓ of the circle ahead of you to help guide your pony.

Diamond

Ride a diamond by meeting the same points that you would on a 20m circle (A, X and the two points where you meet the track), but ride corners and straight lines rather than curves.

Shallow loop

As you come down the long side of the arena, ask for an inside bend and move your pony off the track, then change your bend and straighten up for a few strides. Ask for outside bend again and move back towards the track. As you rejoin the track ask for an inside bend.

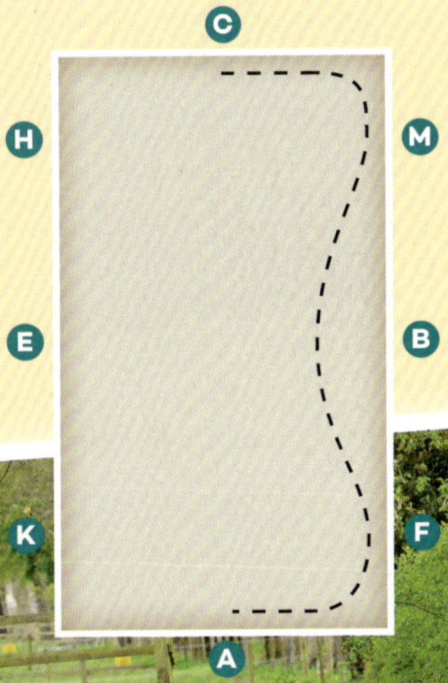

TOP TIP

Try each exercise in walk first.

Figure of eight

A figure of eight is like two 20m circles ridden together, but it's commonly mistaken for two changes of rein across the long diagonal. Remember to change your diagonal at X if you're trotting.

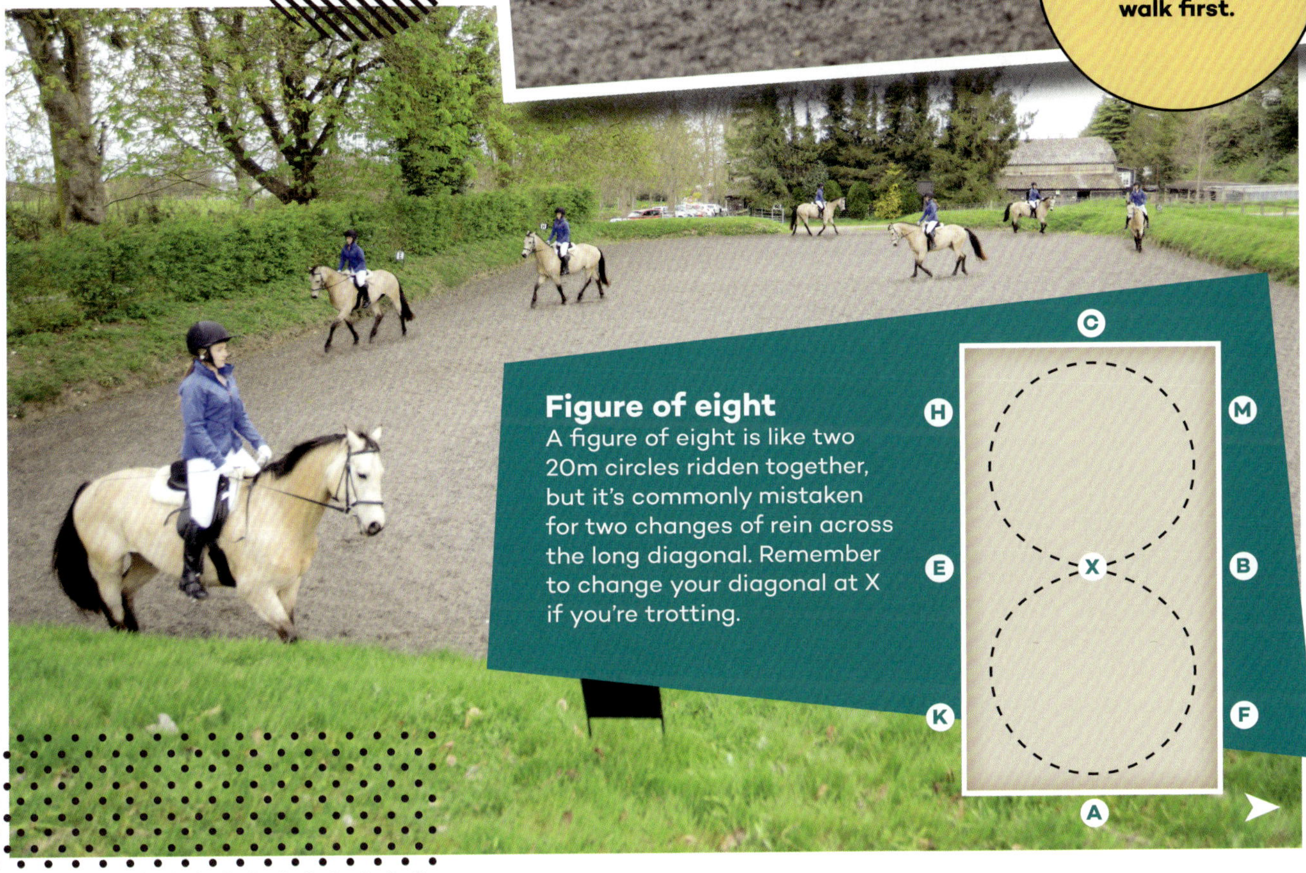

CHANGING DIRECTION

Changes of rein don't have to be boring – there are so many more options than turning down the centre line. Here are some changes of rein you can try...

Long diagonal

This is an easy, wide turn you can use to change the rein before your pony's warmed up. Turn when your body reaches the first marker and ride straight to the next.

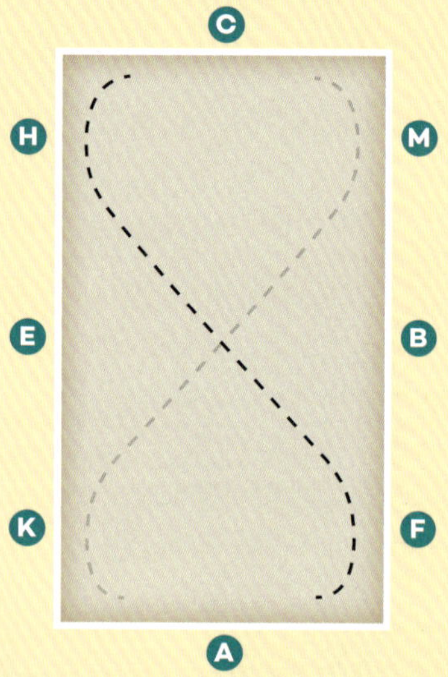

Short diagonal

Very similar to changing the rein across a long diagonal, you can change across the short diagonals, too.

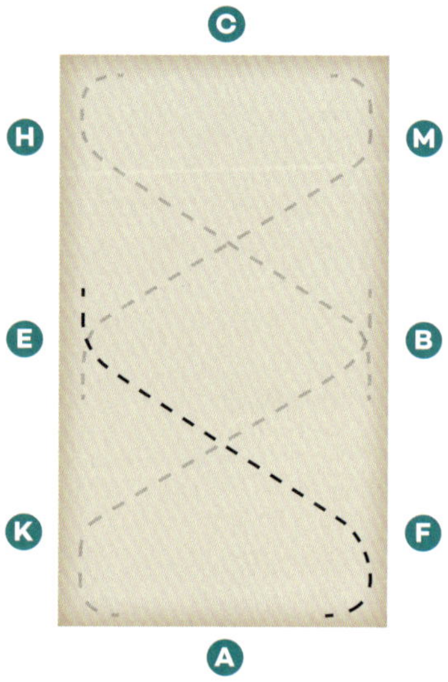

Two half 10m circles

This requires accurate riding to get two equal semi-circles. From E or B, ride a half 10m circle to X, then ride three strides straight, change your bend and ride another half circle back to E or B on the other side of the school.

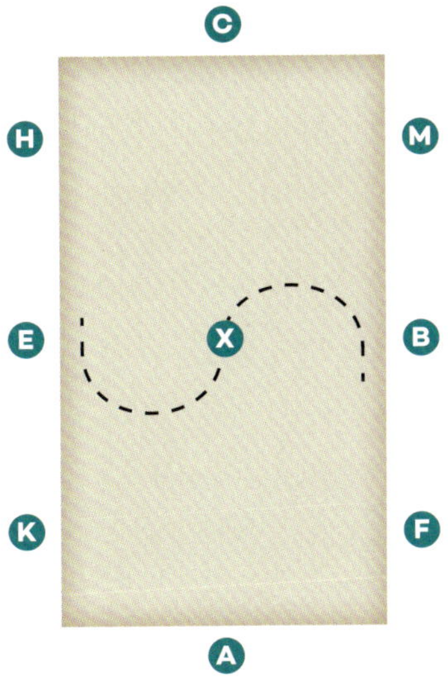

Teardrop

Ride a half 10m circle at H (or M, F, K) and when you reach the centre line ride straight towards E or B, asking for inside bend before you reach the track.

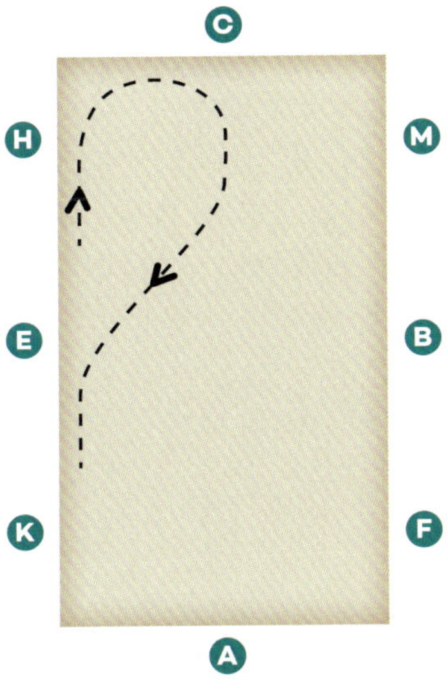

Turn-on-the-forehand

Change the rein on the spot by riding a turn on the forehand. Ask your pony to halt then, keeping his front legs on the same spot, push his hindquarters around.

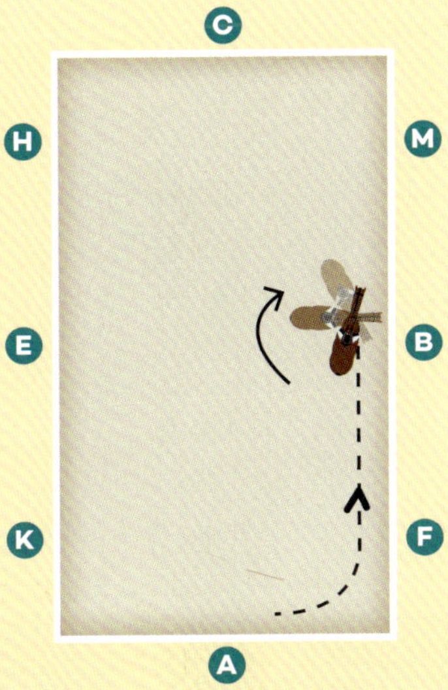

TOP TIP

Save shapes with tight turns until your pony is warmed up.

Four-loop serpentine

Change the rein by turning across the school three times, make sure there's equal spacing between each turn as if you were cutting the school into four quarters. Remember to change your diagonal each time you cross the centre line.

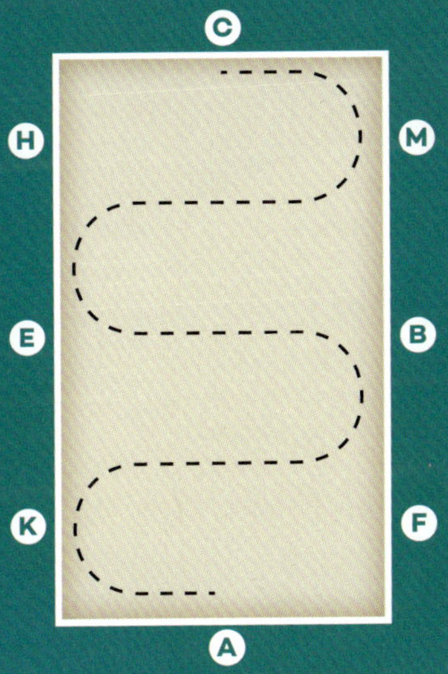

DID YOU KNOW?

You can ride three- and five-loop serpentines, too, but these won't change the rein.

RUG LIKE A PRO!

Can you put a rug on correctly? Our fab how-to guide has all you need to know

From turnouts to coolers, rugs are an essential part of most ponies' wardrobe. Follow these simple steps for perfect rugging, every time...

TOP TIP

Rugs tend to slip back slightly as your pony moves, so start off with it loose around his shoulders so it doesn't rub him.

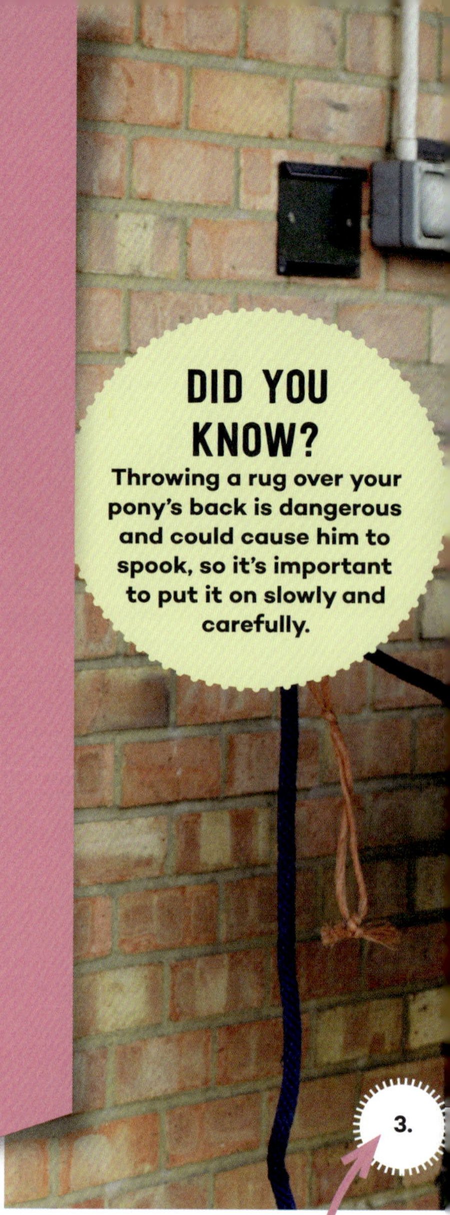

DID YOU KNOW?

Throwing a rug over your pony's back is dangerous and could cause him to spook, so it's important to put it on slowly and carefully.

3.

1. With your pony tied up securely, fold his rug in half so the back section is on top. Place it over his withers so it's sitting straight.

2. Fasten one of the chest straps to keep the rug in place, then unfold the back section over his quarters. The end of the rug should reach the top of his tail.

DID YOU KNOW?

The chest straps are fastened first so the rug can't slip backwards and get tangled in your pony's back legs if he moves.

3. Fasten the other chest strap. You should be able to fit four fingers between the rug and your pony's chest – if you can't, the straps are too tight or the rug is pulled too far back.

DID YOU KNOW?

If the belly straps are too loose, your pony may get his foot caught in them when he lies down.

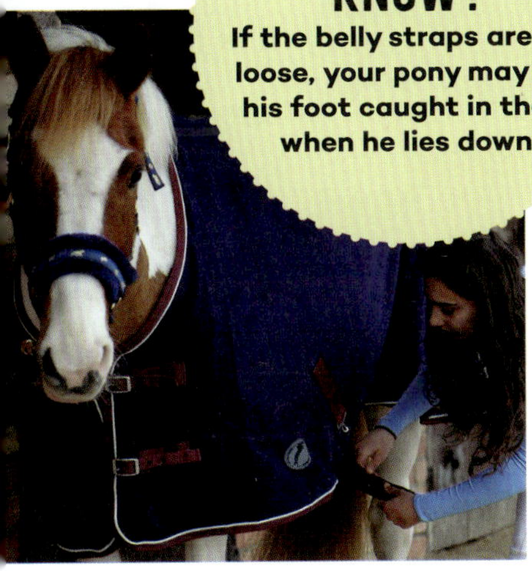

4. Do up the belly straps so they cross over under your pony's tummy. Again, you should be able to fit four fingers between them and his body.

5. Pull his tail through the fillet string. If the rug has leg straps, too, fasten one around his leg on the same side, and then loop the other through before fastening it, too.

Types of rug

- **Turnout rugs** help keep your pony warm and dry when he's in the field. They have a tough, waterproof outer layer and a silky lining. Turnout rugs are usually broken down into lightweight, medium weight and heavyweight, depending on how much filling they have.

- **Cooler rugs** are great for stopping your pony getting a chill if he's worked up a sweat or had a bath. They're often made from fleece or waffle fabric and work by pulling the moisture from his coat and through the rug so it can evaporate away.

- **Stable rugs** are your pony's pyjamas and keep him warm in his stable. They're also great for making sure he stays clean! Like turnout rugs, they come in lightweight, medium weight and heavyweight, so you can choose the perfect thickness whatever the weather.

- **Fly rugs** keep pesky flies and other biting insects off your pony when he's in the field. They're made of mesh, which means they're cool and breathable in warm weather, and often have a piece that wraps around under his belly for extra protection.

TOP TIP

To check if your pony's the right temperature in his rug, put your hand underneath and feel his coat. If he still feels a bit chilly or is starting to sweat, you may need to choose a different rug.

DID YOU KNOW?

If your pony isn't clipped, he may not need to wear a rug at all. Native breeds are designed to live outside in harsh conditions and their thick coats are brilliant at keeping them warm.

Make A PONY PURSE!

Keep your money safe in this super-cute pony purse!

You'll need...

- felt
- needle and thread
- pins
- wool
- scissors
- small piece of ribbon or elastic
- buttons
- googly eyes (optional)
- felt pens (optional)

TOP TIP You may need to ask an adult to help you with the pinning and sewing.

HOW TO DO IT

TURN TO PAGE 101 FOR THE PURSE TEMPLATE

1. Trace or photocopy the template. Draw around it onto a sheet of felt and cut out the pieces that make up the purse – you'll need two back pieces.

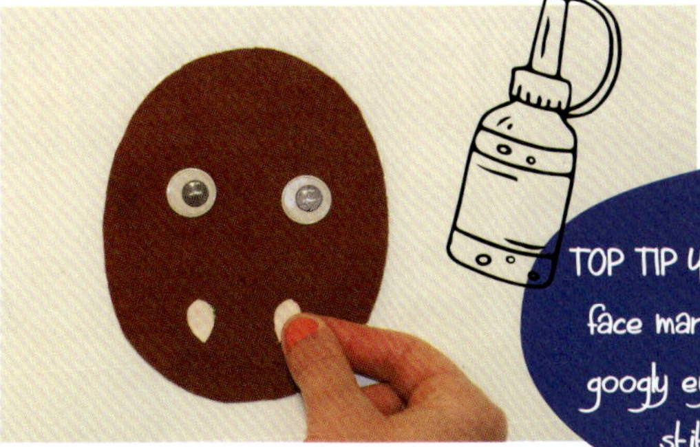

TOP TIP You can either draw on the face markings in felt pen, stick on googly eyes or buttons, or glue or stitch on pieces of felt.

2. Decorate the front piece with eyes, nostrils and even facial markings – why not make it look like your fave pony? **Leave at least 0.5cm of space around the edge to sew the pieces together.**

Use pins to hold the pieces together.

3. Lay the top and bottom back pieces over your pony's face. They should overlap, with the bottom back piece on the top.

4. Using backstitch, sew around the bottom half of your pony's face, then stop when you reach the start of the other back layer.

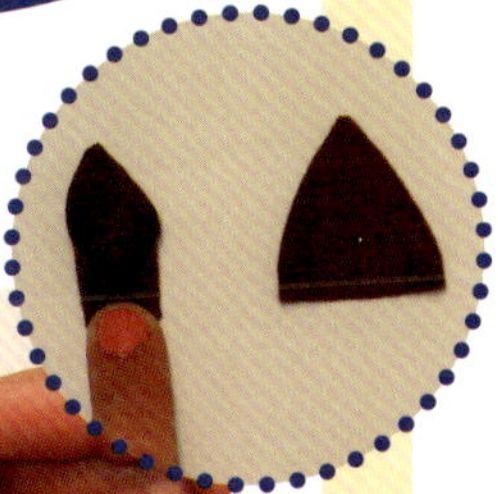

5. Cut out two felt triangles. Fold in the bottom corners to create ears, then pin them inside the felt pieces, pointing down.

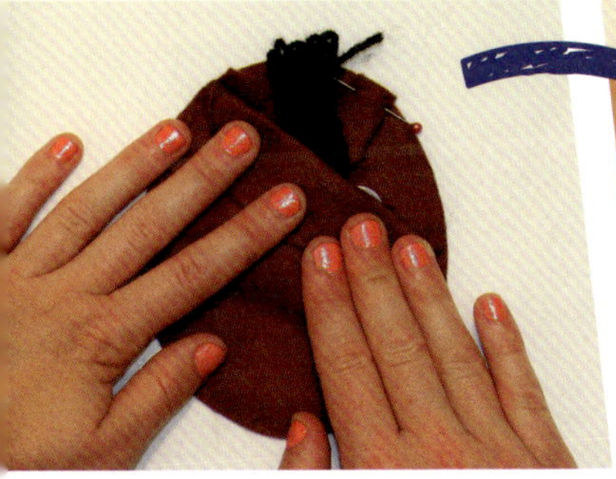

6. Cut some strands of wool for the forelock and pin them between the ears, inside the felt.

7. Continue sewing all the way around the edge of your pony. Tie a knot in the thread and turn him right-side-out, so his face is outside and the edges of the felt are on the inside.

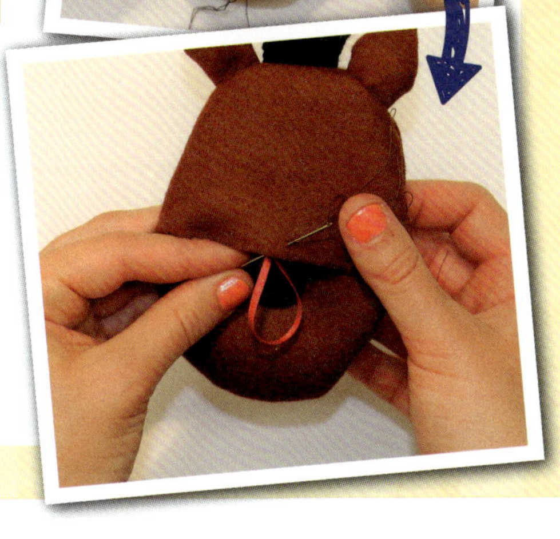

8. For the fastening, sew a button onto the bottom back piece and sew a loop of ribbon or elastic under the flap of the top back piece. Slide the button through the loop to fasten and there you have it – your very own pony purse!

BEST OF BRITISH BREEDS

HIGHLAND

We're off to the north of Scotland to meet the mega Highland pony!

The Highland pony is one of only three breeds native to Scotland, and is one of the largest British pony breeds.

DID YOU KNOW?

The modern Highland pony has been influenced by the addition of Arab blood. This has made the breed larger and given it more stamina – and may have also contributed to its pretty, arched neck!

FAST FACTS

Height: 13–14.2hh
Colour: Known for a mega range of dun shades, including mouse, cream dun, oatmeal and biscuit dun. Grey, brown or black are also common, with bay and chestnut more rarely seen.
Place of origin: The Scottish Highlands and islands
The pony for you if... you have a taste for adventure – Highland ponies can tackle anything from trekking to vaulting!

Highland history

It's tricky to trace the origin of the Highland breed, as two types of pony originally roamed the wilds of Scotland. The first was a lighter, riding pony type, which was found in the Western Isles, and the second, larger type – often referred to as a 'garron' – lived on the mainland. Over time, the two types combined and created the modern Highland pony. The addition of French and Spanish bloodlines, as well as Hackney and Fell influence, helped to form the breed into a reliable farming animal. Highlands were used for ploughing, hauling timber and carrying game back after hunting.

Style guide

Good conformation is a really important part of Highland breed standards. The body is compact and well put together, with a deep girth and sloping shoulder, which allows them to move well under saddle and also to put their strength into driving and pulling. The neck is long and they have a broad-muzzle and kind eye. The mane and tail should be thick and traditionally left untrimmed, and the legs have silky feathers.

DID YOU KNOW?

There are only about 5,500 Highland ponies left in the world, putting them on the 'At Risk' list.

The Highland pony comes from the Scottish Highlands, from which it takes its name, and the Western Isles, including Orkney and Shetland.

Today's talents

Highland ponies are still used in stag and grouse hunting, and are favoured by the Queen for this – she breeds them at Balmoral Castle in Scotland. They're also really popular pony-trekking mounts, as they're sure-footed and reliable, so you can always trust them to keep you safe! Highlands are a popular Pony Club pony, too, because their versatility means they can turn a hoof to all activities, including jumping and mounted games.

FLEX THOSE MUSCLES

Highland ponies can carry a weight of up to 15 stone – impressive stuff!

FOLLOW THE RULES

The Highland Pony Society frowns upon any sort of white markings, other than a small star – white legs and hooves aren't allowed in the show ring. Instead, Highlands have their own cool markings – they often have dorsal stripes and zebra-style markings on their legs!

MY PERFECT ROUTINE

Want to know what it takes to look after a pony? Rachel and Emilio reveal all

1

When I arrive at the yard, my first job (after giving Emilio a quick cuddle!) is to **check his water** trough is full. This is super-important as fresh, clean water keeps him well-hydrated.

2

I catch Emilio and **check his rug**. Thankfully, he hasn't been cheeky and tried to undo any straps today! I also make sure he's a good temperature – not too hot or cold.

3

I bring Emilio to the yard to give him a **groom and thorough check over**. He's always sooooo dirty after being out in the field so it can be hard work, but I love spending quality one-on-one time with him.

4

Now for my fave time of the day – **riding**! I tack up Emilio, and get all my kit on. Today's our chance to perfect some dressage moves, so we're heading for the school.

6

Ugh, it's time for **poo-picking**. Even though I'm not a big fan of the job, it's important to make sure Emilio's field is cleared every day so he doesn't get worms and his paddock doesn't turn sour.

5

I always **clean my tack** after riding so it stays looking super-smart.

7

This is deffo Emilio's favourite part of the day – **feed time**! I love giving him a scratch while I wait for him to empty his bucket.

8

Finally, it's time to **turn him out**. I put Emilio's rug on and let him free to play with his friends! He always canters over to say hello, but then gets stuck into a well-deserved graze!

A MOONLIT ADVENTURE

Harriet never dreamed that her pony, Moonlight, was so special or how he'd change her life forever...

Harriet had a secret that she couldn't tell anybody. Not her mum, or even her best friend, Jessie. It was such an enormous secret that, even if she tried to tell them, they wouldn't believe her. They'd think she'd gone crazy. Harriet knew that once the sun had set for the day and the moon had risen, when everyone else was asleep, all the toys and other still objects would come alive. She'd seen them with her pony, Moonlight.

Moonlight wasn't a normal pony. He was a moon pony. Moon ponies are the keepers of the moon magic, which is responsible for making the toys come to life. Moonlight and all of the other moon ponies make sure that the toys stayed safe while on their night-time adventures. Now, I'm sure you're wondering how Harriet could talk to Moonlight, as obviously ponies can't talk, but moon ponies can talk to humans after dark, once the sun has set and the moon has risen.

Harriet clearly remembered the night she first discovered Moonlight's secret. She'd just come home from a rehearsal for her school play. It was really late, but Harriet couldn't resist going down to the stables to give Moonlight a goodnight kiss.

"I love you Moonie, see you in the morning," she said, giving him a cuddle. "Good night, Harriet," he replied. Harriet couldn't believe her ears. She backed away, staring at him with wide eyes. "You didn't speak, you can't speak, you're a pony!" Moonlight looked straight at her and said kindly, "I can. Not all ponies can talk but I'm a moon pony and we're different."

Just at that moment, Harriet's mum called from the house. Moonlight looked at Harriet, "Go, I'll explain everything another time." Reluctantly she turned and ran back across the garden to the house. That night Harriet tossed and turned, but just couldn't sleep. Finally, she decided she needed some answers, so she crept out of bed, down the stairs, grabbed a coat and her wellies and slipped silently out of the back door.

What's going on?

Harriet ran down the garden to the yard and carefully opened Moonlight's stable door. "Moonie," she called softly, "are you awake? Please can you tell me what's going on? What are moon ponies?" She waited impatiently for him to speak, very worried that she'd imagined him speaking at all. He looked at her hard for a moment, then began to explain.

"Have you ever wondered," Moonlight asked, "why your favourite toy isn't exactly where you left it the night before? You might have been playing with it by the window and when you go back to it the next day, it's not there?" Harriet couldn't believe it. "Yes! That happens all the time!" she exclaimed. "That's because every night, after the moon has risen and everyone's asleep, your toys come alive. They walk, talk and play all through the night, but when the morning comes they have to go back to their homes and become regular toys again."

Harriet took a moment to think. "So, where do you fit into all of this?" she asked. "What's a moon pony? What do they have to do with toys?" Moonlight patiently explained, "Well, it's magic from the moon that brings the toys to life, and moon ponies make sure that the toys are safe so that no one discovers their secret." There was a pause, Harriet was confused. "But if you can't tell anyone why did you tell me?" asked Harriet. "I told you because I need your help," Moonlight said, with a glint in his eye.

Night rescue

Quietly, Harriet tacked up Moonlight and left the yard. They walked in silence for a while, both thinking about what they had to do. Moonlight had told her about a teddy bear who had become stuck in a tree trying to find away across the river, but he couldn't reach him. After about 10 minutes of walking they came across the bear, hanging from a snag in his stitching high up in an oak tree.

"Right, how can I help?" said Harriet, looking up at the stranded bear. "Well..." Moonlight replied, "I thought that you might be able to kneel on my back, reach up and grab poor Ted." Harriet thought for a minute. "Okay, I'll try, but you've got to stay really still." Moonlight nodded and got into position under the branch. "You need to go forward a few steps Moonie... now stop. That's perfect." Being very careful to keep her balance, Harriet slowly got to her knees on Moonlight's saddle and stretched up, trying to reach the poor stranded bear.

> "Moonlight is no ordinary pony"

"It's no good, Harriet, you're going to have to stand. I promise I won't move a muscle!" Moonlight said after watching her struggle. Very slowly Harriet stood up on the saddle. Taking deep, calming breaths she managed to keep her balance, then carefully reach up to the bear. "Come on," Harriet called to Ted, "You've got to help me. See if you can wriggle closer to the end of the branch." Ted looked nervous. "I'll try," he answered, "I've been stuck here for two days. My human, Tommy, is going to be so worried."

Moonlight and Harriet watched with baited breath as Ted managed to slide himself along the branch until he couldn't get any further. "That's good, I'm going to see if I can get you down now," said Harriet as she once again grabbed for him. Balancing on her tiptoes, she managed to get him free. Harriet carefully climbed down off Moonlight's saddle and onto the ground. "Thank you, thank you, thank you!" Ted said, jumping up and down in excitement. "Tommy's going to be so relieved to have me back. I know he'll have been sick with worry." Moonlight smiled softly. "That's okay," he replied, "but we need to get you back to him, and there's not much of the night left. Ride with Harriet and we'll take you home to Tommy."

Harriet remounted while tightly holding Ted, and Moonlight took off through the woods, faster that Harriet had ever felt him gallop. Eventually they arrived at a little ivy-covered cottage and Moonlight slowed.

"Quickly now, Ted, scramble up the ivy and through the window." Harriet helped him onto the branches of the vine and watched as he nimbly climbed through the open window.

"Harriet, we've got to get back before anyone realises we're missing. I need you to close your eyes tight, I'm going to use the moonlight to transport us back. This takes a lot of energy and concentration, so I need you to be as still and quiet as possible." She agreed, closed her eyes, stroked his neck, and the next thing she knew they were back in his stable. "It's time to go back to the house," Moonlight whispered. Harriet quickly took off his tack, gave him a quick hug and carefully let herself through the back door.

Back to normal

The next morning Harriet was exhausted. At first she was sure she had dreamt the whole thing, but then when she went out to the yard, Harriet noticed Moonlight had dried sweat patches where his tack had been the night before and she knew it had to be true. Ever since that night, she and Moonlight have been working as a team to help look after wandering toys who have become stuck or lost while on their night-time adventures. So if you ever come across a lost-looking teddy bear or a seemingly abandoned toy, remember that they might just be waiting for Harriet and Moonlight to help them get back home.

THE ANSWERS

Page 22

WHAT'S THAT?

1. B
2. A
3. A
4. C
5. B
6. A
7. C
8. A
9. B
10. C

Page 64

WHAT DOES THAT MEAN?

1. Gaskin
2. Withers
3. Pastern
4. Croup
5. Chestnut
6. Hanoverian
7. Clydesdale
8. Icelandic
9. Irish Draught
10. Akhal-Teke
11. A
12. B
13. B
14. A
15. C

Page 54

WHAT COLOUR'S THAT?

Match the markings

1. A – 2
B – 3
C – 4
D – 1

2. A – 3
B – 4
C – 1
D – 2

Correct colours

3. A – Black
B – Grey
C – Bay
D – Chestnut

4. A – Piebald
B – Palomino
C – Strawberry roan
D – Appaloosa

The lightning round

5. Wall eye
6. Dorsal stripe
7. Roan
8. False, Haflingers are chestnut with a flaxen mane and tail
9. True
10. False, most grey ponies are born black, bay or chestnut, and their coat gradually lightens as they get older
11. Chestnut
12. Whorl

Page 80

WHAT'S THE PROBLEM?

● **Problem 1 – B**
Splints can appear when the splint bone or area around it is damaged.

● **Problem 2 – C**
Mud fever is a skin infection that occurs when wet conditions have softened your pony's skin, allowing bacteria in.

● **Problem 3 – B**
Sweet itch is an allergic reaction to the bite of the *Culicoides* midge.

● **Problem 4 – A**
Laminitis occurs when the laminae inside your pony's hooves become inflamed, which can cause permanent damage to his feet. If your pony has laminitis, it's an emergency.

● **Problem 5 – C**
Colic is when your pony has pain in his abdomen, which can be caused by lots of different things. If he has colic, he needs to see the vet straightaway.

● **Problem 6 – B**
PPID is a hormonal disease that's normally seen in older ponies. It's caused by changes to the pituitary gland at the base of your pony's brain.

● **Problem 7 – A**
An overreach is a wound to the bulb of your pony's heel on his front foot caused by him treading on it with his hind foot.

● **Problem 8 – C**
A sarcoid is a form of skin tumour. They're really common and there are several different types.

● **Problem 9 – C**
Sunburn can occur when pink areas of your pony's skin, which have no built-in sun protection, have been exposed to too much sun.

● **Problem 10 – A**
Thrush is an infection in your pony's frog caused by bacteria and fungus.

8–10 right answers = Pony health guru!
You're super clued-up on all things veterinary and nothing unusual about your pony goes unnoticed. You're the person everyone on the yard goes to for advice if they're worried about their pony. Keep up the good work, your pony couldn't be in better hands!

5–7 right answers = Symptom savvy
You certainly know lots about pony health, but there's still a little room for improvement. Keep an eye out for the vet features in PONY mag to help you brush up on your skills and you'll be a pony health guru before you know it!

1–4 right answers = Building on the basics
Oh dear, it looks like your veterinary knowledge needs a bit of work! There's lots to learn about ponies, but don't worry, you'll pick it up in no time. Spend lots of time watching your pony and checking him over to help you notice when something's not right.

Make

TEMPLATES

Page 40

PONY CAKE

Draw the grid to size on an A4 piece of paper and copy the horse shape.

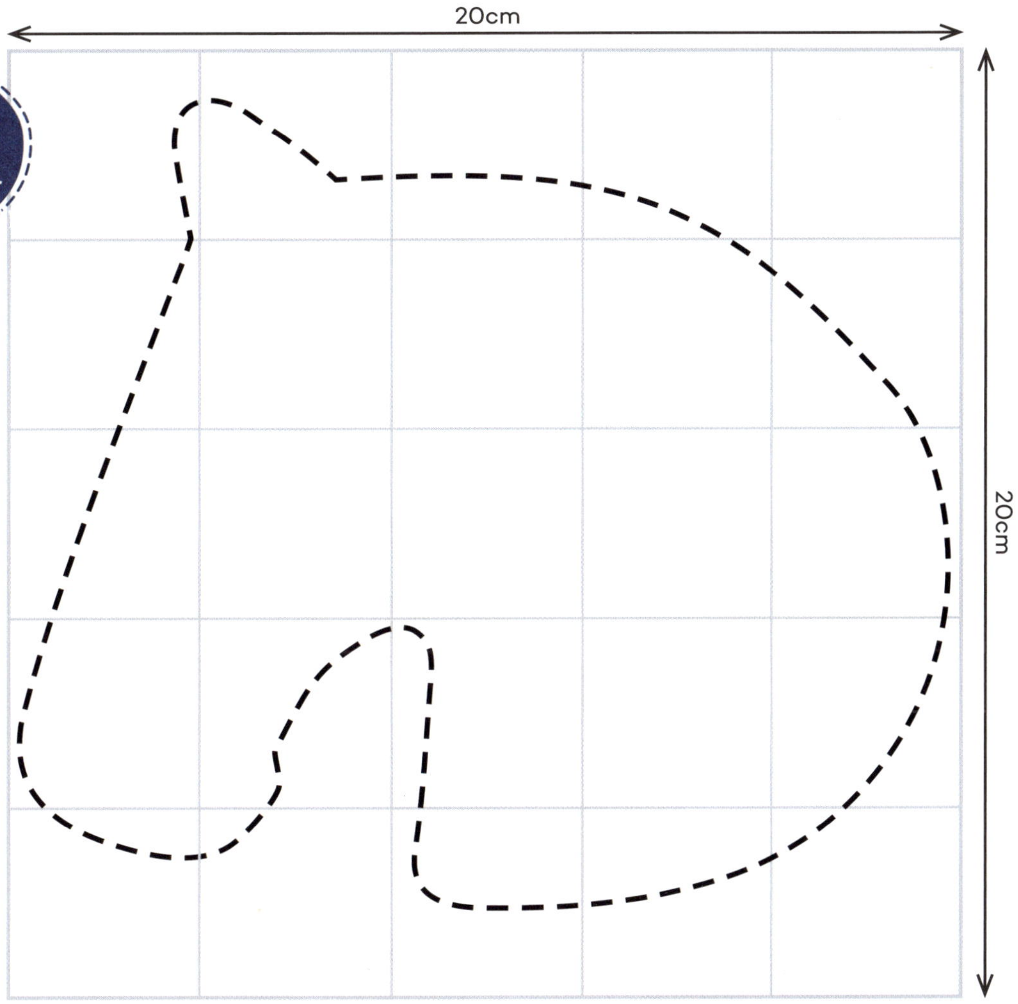

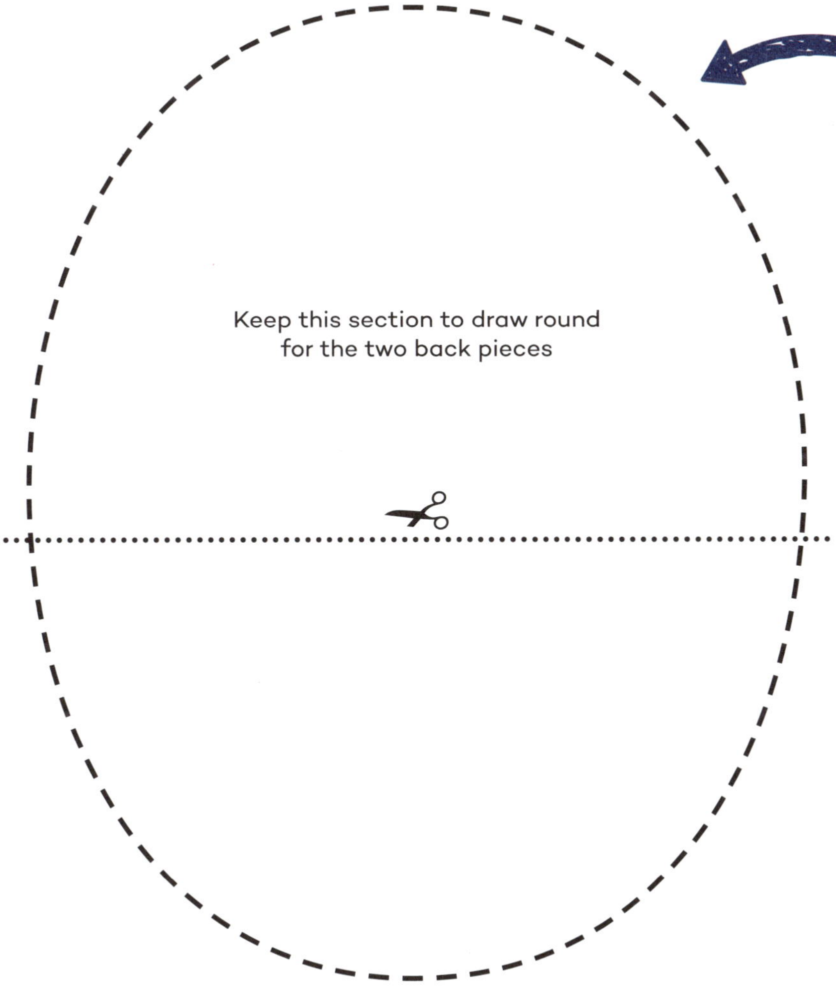

Page 92

PONY PURSE

Trace the template opposite twice. Cut one of your templates in two along the dotted line and keep the larger top section. This is for the two back pieces of the purse.

Photography Bob Atkins **Cover photo** Bob Atkins **Pages 6–7** Land Rover Burghley Horse Trials/Julia Shearwood, Land Rover Burghley Horse Trials, FEI/Arnd Bronkhorst, FEI/Arnd Bronkhorst/Pool Pic, Kit Houghton, Mitsubishi Motors Badminton Horse Trials/Kit Houghton **Pages 20–21** FEI/Christophe Tanière **Pages 42–43** Kevin Owen of digitalworksltd.co.uk **Pages 48–49** Centrill Media/Shutterstock.com **Pages 50–51** FEI/Richard Julliart, Werner and Tammo Ernst, Stefano Grasso/LGCT, Mitch Gunn/Shutterstock.com, Kit Houghton **Pages 56–57** Hippo Foto – Dirk Caremans, FEI/Jon Stroud, Kit Houghton, Arnd Bronkhorst **Pages 70–71** Margo Harrison/Shutterstock.com, Mark William Penny/Shutterstock.com **Page 80** Bob Langrish **Pages 94–95** Toni Cadwell, Suzanne Punnett, Lesley Dawson **Pages 102–103** Illustrations by Helena Öhmark and Rebecca Öhmark

THE MISADVENTURES OF CHARLIE!